T0273682

THE GREAT

RESIGNATION

THE GREAT

RESIGNATION

How Coaching and Appreciative
Leadership Can Help You Win
the War for Talent

LAURA DARRELL

NEW YORK

LONDON • NASHVILLE • MELBOURNE • VANCOUVER

The Great Resignation

How Coaching and Appreciative Leadership Can Help You Win the War for Talent

© 2024 Laura Darrell

Published in New York, New York, by Morgan James Publishing. Morgan James is a trademark of Morgan James, LLC. www.MorganJamesPublishing.com

Proudly distributed by Publishers Group West®

Morgan James BOGO™

A **FREE** ebook edition is available for you or a friend with the purchase of this print book.

CLEARLY SIGN YOUR NAME ABOVE

Instructions to claim your free ebook edition:
1. Visit MorganJamesBOGO.com
2. Sign your name CLEARLY in the space above
3. Complete the form and submit a photo of this entire page
4. You or your friend can download the ebook to your preferred device

ISBN 9781636983615 paperback
ISBN 9781636983622 ebook
Library of Congress Control Number: 2023952328

Cover Design by:
FormattedBooks
www.formattedbooks.com

Interior Design by:
FormattedBooks
www.formattedbooks.com

Morgan James is a proud partner of Habitat for Humanity Peninsula and Greater Williamsburg. Partners in building since 2006.

Get involved today! Visit: www.morgan-james-publishing.com/giving-back

CONTENTS

PART ONE—WHY THEY LEAVE

PART TWO—CLOSING THE CULTURE GAP

THE GREAT RESIGNATION

The post-COVID world has seen the highest number of employee resignations since they started tracking this data in the year 2000.[1] Employees are tired of organizations that make them feel undervalued, underdeveloped, underappreciated, and ultimately uncared for by their managers. COVID-19 and its disruption of work patterns allowed people to re-evaluate their working conditions and change what matters most to them. While this is a good thing for employees, better aligning their values and principles with a new organization, it has been tremendously disruptive for employers worldwide. What was good enough for employees yesterday is simply not cutting it in today's competitive labor market. At the time of writing this book, both the US and Canada are experiencing near-record low unemployment rates, with specific industries suffering more than others.[2,3] As hospitality and tourism started their long road to recovery in the post-COVID world, they desperately needed to rehire employees at breakneck speeds to meet a robust return to normal in those sectors. Customer expectations did not decrease in this new world, and a society that had largely stayed home for the past two years was desperate to return to life. Add to this the strain healthcare systems are under to fill critical vacancies worldwide and the chronic IT workforce shortages that have plagued that sector for years, and you have a recipe for significant workforce planning issues.[4,5]

Previously, employees who valued job security were less likely to change companies; however, the new reality is that continued pressure on the labor market has changed the game. More than ever, employees are being tempted by headlines about the low unemployment and stiff competition to hire workers and are checking out other opportunities. How you attracted and retained employees in the pre-COVID era isn't going to retain your existing workforce, let alone attract new employees to your vacant roles. Today, on average, organizations take over forty days to fill their vacant roles[6]; with an increase in the time required to hire or replace an employee, working short-handed is negatively affecting the rest of the organization. Consider the impact of turnover on the employees who have to cover the workload for vacant positions or how your customer experience may suffer while someone is working double duty—not a good result in a battered post-COVID-19 economy. Ultimately, this can have a spiral-down effect on your remaining workforce, often causing more turnover.

However, now isn't the time for panic; winning the war for talent is in your hands. Some of the best employers in the world today, like HSBC, Neutrogena, KLM, Starbucks, Thomson Reuters, Pal's Burgers, and Virgin Atlantic, are experiencing low turnover even today.[7,8,9] Their results prove that during this challenging hiring environment, creating a working culture that attracts and retains your industry's best and brightest talent is still possible.

Illuminating the Problem

For many years, leadership relied on principles of a bygone era to manage their workforce, predominantly using tactics from a "command and control" or "authoritarian" leadership style. One needs only to look at the mandated "return to the office" approach taken by many organizations as a good example of this leadership style. But as the boomers and their "military-centric" leadership style retire the workforce, many from Generation X are taking the helm. The challenge is that leaders today are inheriting outdated management systems and a workplace culture that makes it difficult to attract and retain top talent. They rely on the notion the paycheck is reward enough to keep their team members engaged. The great resignation has exasperated these systemic issues; employees want and expect more from their employers, and if they don't get it, they can and will go elsewhere. Leadership and executive teams worldwide must take a hard look at what types of incentives and working environments they offer their employees and how that experience impacts their overall recruitment and retention efforts. They need to heed their findings, listen to their employees, and take the necessary action to change their programs, systems, and tools.

What will you learn?

Employee engagement isn't what many people assume it is. Salary and benefits are essential, but today, they are considered table stakes, the bare minimum required for someone to consider an employment opportunity with your organization. Employees today expect to be paid at the market or above salary level for their region, have benefits for themselves and their families, have the ability to work in a hybrid office environment, and have some employer-specific perks. For example, suppose your business is in the restaurant or hotel industry. In that case, individual employees might naturally expect a meal or hotel stay program as part of their overall compensation package. Total salary isn't usually the problem; the other things that matter immensely to people, specifically millennials and Generation Z, are missing. I'm talking about appreciation, recognition, career progression, a culture of development, and coaching. A recent survey of millennials and Generation Z conducted by Deloitte found that an environment where these cohorts can learn and develop their skills, having an opportunity to advance their career and earn more money, is one of the most important items on their new employer wish list.[10]

This book is for all people managers at all levels of an organization, those who actively lead in any capacity, hybrid or fully remote, regardless of team size. The tactics put forward concerning attracting and retaining top talent are practical, can be quickly adopted, and cost little to no money to implement. You read that right. They cost little to no money to implement, and they will profoundly impact your team's happiness and the overall health of your organization. You'll build a deep bench of talent ready to take on more and different responsibilities. You'll foster better relationships with your employees and customers and ultimately win the war for talent.

Where did these strategies come from?

During a career that spanned over twenty-five years, working at some of North America's most iconic and beloved brands, like Starbucks, Apple, A&W, Workopolis (now Indeed.com), and Boston Pizza International, I had the opportunity to learn from some of the best leaders in their respective industries. I studied them and the processes they used to identify, nurture, and advance top talent. I spent years developing people, teams, and departments using those tools and techniques, leading to more successful team member promotions than I can recall. I channeled my focus to personal and professional development. I built systems around performance reviews, development planning, and internal promotions that were best in class, and I had the results to prove it. My turnover was well below my peers' and the industry average for managers and entry-level positions. I had the highest number of internal promotions and a culture that attracted the best and brightest. My "boots on the ground" experience and my formal leadership education have enabled me to design programs that work. These programs have been tried, tested, and enhanced by some of the best leaders I've had the privilege of working alongside.

Turning This Book into Action

We all know that great ideas are just that—great ideas. They don't turn into great results unless acted upon; the secret to change is to have a plan and to work on that plan every day. EVERY. SINGLE. DAY. In each section of *The Great Resignation*, you will find reflective questions that will help you identify areas of opportunity that can be used to chart your course. The resource section showcases all the templates you need to execute these programs with your teams, your department, or the entire organization, and you can download them for free at www.thegreatresignationtoolkit.com. We'll cap things off with a section on change leadership because, as I said, ideas are great, but getting them implemented in your organization is the only way to see the results, and let's face it, sometimes change is hard.

So I thank you for joining me on this journey to enhance the day-to-day working experience for as many people as possible. Leadership can profoundly impact people's lives, and I'm excited to hear your stories about how this book helped you attract and retain your best and brightest team members. Be well, friends.

Laura Darrell - MA Leadership
Speaker | Leadership Coach |
Former Operations Executive

PART ONE

Why They Leave

1

LACK OF CAREER OPPORTUNITIES

Nothing is more important than hiring and developing people.
At the end of the day, you bet on people, not strategies.
Lawrence Bossidy, former COO of General Electric

Recent workplace studies have found that over 60 percent of employees would stay in their jobs for three years longer if they felt like their company and managers cared about and were invested in their professional development and helped them work toward career progression goals.[11] Similarly, most exit interviews and studies about why people leave their jobs find a lack of career opportunities often tops the list. The reality is people want to learn and be developed, knowing they'll have an opportunity to advance in their careers, earn more money, and do more challenging work.

There is an undue amount of focus put on salary as the main driver for employee satisfaction and how people prioritize what matters most in finding their next job, but this is an old paradigm. The Millennial Generation and Generation Z who follow them are far more likely to cite coaching, development, and mentorship as ideal working environments than any other generation.[12],[13] I'm not suggesting salary and benefits are unimportant; if you find yourself with total compensation below your industry average, you will struggle to compete for talent. With tools like Glassdoor and PayScale, it's much easier for people to figure out their region's high, mean, and low salaries and negotiate accordingly. Things like recognition, coaching, and development factor in when the basic compensation and benefits needs are met.

A career spent leading large teams and business units taught me to highly value a business principle that helped to nurture internal talent, ensuring they had room to grow. I call it the 80/20 rule, aiming for 80 percent of promotions to come from internal candidates and the other 20 percent to come externally. This principle helps to ensure, first and foremost, your team believes there is room for them to advance. It also ensures some opportunity still exists for external talent to join the organization. Don't get me wrong; external skills are vital to all organizations. These team members can help you look at your business through a different lens, challenge the status quo, and mitigate the ultimate kiss of business death, the "we've always done it this way" approach. Like most things in life, ensuring balance in your internal promotions and external hires is essential.

An excellent place to start living this principle in your organization is simply to post your open positions internally. Doing so enables you to gauge the interest of your existing team members, understanding if there is a qualified candidate you could consider before looking outside of the organization. Allowing candidates to apply internally also creates valuable interview experience, feedback, and coaching should they not be successful with their application. The feedback from an unsuccessful interview can often yield very specific areas to focus their future development efforts on, increasing the possibility they will succeed in their next attempt. To facilitate the likelihood an internal candidate will be ready for consideration, bringing your departments together twice per year to discuss the top performers and their readiness level for moving up or taking on new roles within the organization is a good best practice. This can help create a line of sight to the organization's top talent, which is essential when building a solid bench of internal candidates. Hosting these meetings with other department leaders can highlight available talent throughout the organization. For example, you may have individuals in your department who could be suitable for a role or assignment within a different business unit. Opening these channels of communication is essential to the people-planning process. Conversely, you may have a team member struggling in their role and likely not to make it; knowing far in advance who you have on the bench in other areas of the business who might step into that role can help with your planning and timing.

Often, managers relate "growth" to promotion, but this is far from accurate. More than anything, your team members want an opportunity to learn new skills that help round out their current professional experience. Things like role secondment into another department for short-term or long-term assignments and lateral moves into different parts of the organization are excellent ways to show pathways to growth. Often overlooked, this approach has many benefits, especially in the retail and hospitality sectors. Consider the positive impact of cross-training your team members to work in other parts of the business or department. It helps to ensure that when the team member is ready to hit that next level in their career, they have a much more robust understanding of the business instead of a one-dimensional view.

Another benefit to having an internal promotion and cross-training strategy in your business is its significant impact on your teams' morale. When people see their peers getting promoted or moving laterally to gain new experience in a different department or big project, it can excite and motivate them. It shows them the "promote from within" culture you talked about in your recruitment messaging, interviews, and orientations is more than words. They come to life in tangible ways that every team member can see—leaders walking the walk!

The other significant benefit to focusing on internal talent movement is that the time to ramp up in their new role is measurably less. Team members who advance internally usually hit the ground running in their new roles much faster.[14] Of course, unique parts of the job will take time to learn and master, but they already have a significant leg up—they know the culture and how the business works. There is an old saying in the recruiting world: hire for culture and train the rest. Culture is difficult to assess during the hiring process. Internal promotions have already shown that not only do they know and understand the culture, but chances are, because you're considering promoting them, they've already demonstrated they're a good fit for your organization.

It's also essential to contemplate the impact of a culture of internal promotion on those considering accepting a job offer with your organization. Potential new employees are far more likely to want to work at a company with a proven track record of developing and promoting internal talent than a company that can't provide any examples of recent internal promotions. Or, worse yet, one that has high turnover and an obvious retention problem. Job seekers are far more intelligent than we think. If they see that you are always hiring for the same type of role and frequently have many job postings open compared to the size of your company, they may worry that you have retention issues and people don't want to work there. Internal promotions demonstrate to the candidate that your organization values hard work and you are willing to reward such behavior.

Finally, having a culture that values your team members' contributions while encouraging them to strive for internal promotions or other development opportunities can also impact your consumer brand. We often don't draw a correlation between our reputation as an employer and how our customers might view us. Recent studies on employer branding and its impact on consumer brands have shown that as high as 64 percent of customers have stopped buying a product, using a service, or visiting a store or restaurant because of how their employees are treated.[15] What better way to show your employees you value them and their contributions than to have a strong focus on their development and career progression?

CHAPTER ONE
REFLECTIVE QUESTIONS

1. How often does your organization promote internal candidates or cross-train team members to work in other departments? Who are the most recent examples?

   _____

   _____

   _____

2. Does your organization pay salaries or wages at or above the regional market average? Search for your competitors on Glassdoor or Payscale to check and compare.

   _____

   _____

   _____

3. How many team members have left your organization in the past twelve months? Do you know why they left? List the most recent ones below.

_____

_____

_____

4. Do you have thoughtfully crafted development plans for all your top performers? What follow-up routine do you use to measure and monitor progress?

_____

_____

_____

2

NO INVESTMENT IN COACHING OR DEVELOPMENT

The only thing worse than training your employees and having them leave is not training them and having them stay.

Henry Ford

A staggering number of employees, over 70 percent, have suggested they lack the skills and have not had adequate training to execute their job duties.[16] Perhaps even more shocking is a study conducted by West Monroe Partners, a US national management consulting firm, which found most American managers have received no management training.[17] Such a significant gap in leadership training is alarming and paints a bleak picture of the experience for the team members working under these managers and the likelihood they will stay with the organization. According to a poll conducted by Gallup of over one million American workers, the main reason people quit their jobs was because of a bad manager.[18] These statistics help highlight the urgent need for all team members and those who lead them to undergo standardized training programs. The benefits could be many.

When your new hires experience a robust training program, it immediately enhances their overall knowledge and skills related to their job, leading to a higher level of confidence in their ability to get the job done effectively and efficiently. A robust onboarding and training experience also shines a light on your company's goals, values, and working culture. Team members who feel connected to the organization and its goals are more likely to experience job satisfaction and want to stay.[19] When team members in the same or similar roles experience the same approach to training and the same content, it can directly impact consistency, and consistency is essential for the overall success of any organization.[20] A lack of consistency in employee performance can negatively impact your customer experience, product wastage, and the amount of supervision your team members need, affecting your organization's fiscal performance and negatively impacting your culture. When employees lack proper training, a full 40 percent leave within their first year, resulting in more hiring and training and additional workloads spread among your existing team while the new people get up to speed.[21] Investing in people's training and onboarding signals to your new hires they are valued and you care about their experience working as a part of your company.

Training comes in many forms, and using the right approach when building your training systems and tools is essential. For example, when training new regional managers, I often relied heavily on techniques that delivered knowledge about the entire customer experience and the operating systems required to execute that experience. I also relied on an on-the-job mentorship program with up to three other regional managers so the new team members could see firsthand how their roles came to life in various real-world situations. For example, a restaurant struggling to execute the operating systems would have a different level of engagement and support from its regional manager compared to a restaurant that is achieving great results following all the standardized programs, systems, and tools. This hands-on experience becomes invaluable when the new team member is ready to "go live" in their region.

Considering the content and duration required to get your new employees up to speed quickly and efficiently is essential. First, you must evaluate the hard skills necessary to complete the job. You would put things like product and system knowledge, specific technology and process needed to execute the job, and administrative tools and techniques in this bucket. The second bucket to consider is the soft skills required to perform the job at a high level. This type of training can be a little trickier to execute, and I've often found that mentorship and job shadowing are two of the best methods that deliver results. Another benefit of this training style is the expedited rate that it helps the new team members build relationships on the team and within the organization. Consider this style for aspects related to culture, leadership philosophy, and hands-on practical "day-in-the-life training."

My final word on training would be this: training is precisely that—training the core functions and tasks required to do the job. Training should not be confused with practice; practice happens once the initial training is complete and the new team member is on their own. Based on how they performed during training and what skills and abilities they brought to the job, each team member will require different lengths of time to practice and build their confidence. Ensuring that you have a buddy system in place during this time of practice will help them as they apply their new knowledge. Your new hires will need someone to go to when they inevitably forget an element of their training or encounter their first set of problems or challenges. They may need additional training or support, and the buddy system ensures you wrap your new hires in a safety net during the all-important first ninety days as you help them build skills and foster strong relationships, enabling them to assimilate much quicker into the culture.

Most millennials suggest that further development in their current position is critical to their overall job satisfaction.[22] Generation Z has very similar sentiments.[23] Not delivering in this area could have serious and far-reaching impacts on your ability to attract bright new talent and retain the talent you already have. These folks are passionate about advancing their careers and see professional and personal development as the holy grail of making it happen. Considering the significant number of managers who received no formal training when they began leading people and teams and the complete lack of investment in hybrid or remote leadership skills in the post-COVID world, it's unsurprising that many organizations are having issues in the age of the *great resignation.*

Two leadership styles resonate most with the millennials and Gen Z—a coaching leadership style and an appreciative leadership style. Coaching is the pathway to professional development. With some planning, training, and support from the company's senior leaders, you can get started developing coaching and appreciative leaders almost immediately with very little financial investment. Paying close attention to "proximity bias," a common leadership misconception that in-office workers are more productive and committed than their remote counterparts, is essential to ensuing all employees have equal access to upward career mobility.

So, if we already know how important coaching and development are to the younger workforce, why are so many companies struggling to find and keep great talent? Why are so many from these generational cohorts leaving for what they hope to be greener pastures on the other side? There's no way to sugarcoat this; the truth is the truth. Many organizations don't invest in training and development for their workforce because instead of looking at it as an investment, they consider it an unnecessary cost in the name of higher profits. This thinking is outrageously outdated and a huge reason the younger generations are quitting their jobs in droves. In the wake of so much research and data, inaction at this point is inexcusable. For example, research conducted by Right Management, a global expert in helping organizations retain top talent, found that 70 percent of all organizations surveyed agreed that turnover hurts financial results.[24] According to HR Magazine, 24 percent of employers who spent $1,500 or more on employee development costs had a 24 percent higher profit than those who spent less.[25] Finally, research conducted by HR.org found a 10 percent increase in team member developmental activity yielded an additional 8.6 percent in productivity.[26] Honestly, the research is clear: invest in developing your people; not only will it help you attract and retain top talent, but it will also help you be more profitable—another win-win!

CHAPTER TWO
REFLECTIVE QUESTIONS

1. Does your organization have formalized onboarding plans to welcome new team members to the organization? How is senior leadership involved?

   _____

   _____

   _____

2. How does your organization train the "hard skills" required to execute specific tasks vs. the soft skills needed to build and maintain relationships?

   _____

   _____

   _____

3. How would your daily actions change if you put the development and coaching of your team first?

_____

_____

_____

4. How does your organization measure consistency? Do your current training programs support delivering a consistent experience for your customers?

_____

_____

_____

3

MIDDLE MANAGERS LACK LEADERSHIP TRAINING

*Management is about persuading people to do things they
do not want to do, while leadership is about inspiring
people to do things they never thought they could.*
Steve Jobs

The leaders working in the middle of your organization have
one of the most challenging roles and responsibilities, making
it most concerning to know that many organizations offer little
or no training on even the most fundamental people leadership practices. Considering how much of your workforce,
including the incredibly important frontlines, work for those
middle managers, it's unsurprising that their lack of leadership

knowledge and practice drives many employees to seek employment elsewhere. Over time, middle managers have been given a bad rap. As McKinsey notes in their interesting look at the Vanishing Middle Manager, the era of COVID-19 has not been kind to this cohort, seeing it eliminated or downsized in many organizations.[27] Perhaps if more senior leaders had invested time genuinely trying to understand the critical importance of these roles and then invested in their development, including their ability to lead hybrid or remote teams, a large portion of the great resignation could have been stalled, and a vast pipeline of internal talent would have become visible.

Middle managers, or middle leaders, as I'll address them from here on in, have several critical functions in the organization, none more important than that of a connector. They need to work hard to please two very different stakeholder groups as they are both a leader of their teams and a follower of their leader above them. In a nutshell, this means they need to diplomatically feed their teams' concerns up to the senior leaders in the organization while bringing the feedback and direction from those senior leaders back down into the trenches in a way that isn't soul-crushing to the people doing the frontline work. These are tricky skills to master, especially if you haven't had formal training or an accurate job description outlining this specific purpose. Learning to look up and down the organization while being empathetic to both groups' needs is important. I've seen many middle leaders go wrong here, working too hard to please the top of the hierarchy while barking down orders at those in the trenches. Not only does this not create a positive working environment, but it does little to build awareness and consensus around shared problems and goals.

Being a skilled liaison is a critical function of being a middle leader. A good liaison can masterfully create healthy conversations between people at different levels of the organization who often hold different views and have different timelines and priorities. Because this is often the case in hierarchical organizations, you can appreciate this skill set's importance. Middle leaders who are great liaisons can act as a translator between the two levels of the organization when it comes to helping them understand both groups' goals, problems, and needs. Without awareness of how each group is experiencing day-to-day life, it becomes almost impossible to identify gaps and work to fix them. It can also become tricky to work on the needs of the business, such as the strength of your training and development programs, if your senior leaders aren't aware of their frontline team members' desire to grow or their potential need for additional training and skill development.

Perhaps the most critical area of the middle leaders' responsibility within the organization is to be a conduit between the frontline team members and those who work hard above them in the organization's hierarchy to create the systems and tools used to deliver a product or service to your customers. These frontline folks are who I like to call "closest to the fire," and without them, your business wouldn't come to life. Staying close to these folks and how they are experiencing the company is critical. They will often know long before others in the organization that there is a problem with the products or tools and how it directly or indirectly impacts your customers. But often, senior leaders are so far removed from those on the frontlines that they rely solely on what the middle leaders tell them—or don't—about the situation. A precarious proposition.

If you want to build a bench of strong, capable middle leaders, consider those working on your organization's frontlines. They could make excellent candidates for your talent pipeline for these roles and many others. Stop and consider for a moment the value that someone who talks to your customers all day, every day, could have within different departments in your company. What impact could they have on the research and development process for new products and services for your customers? Or consider the knowledge and experience they could bring to the team that deals with customer satisfaction issues. It's worth the effort to find creative ways to cross-pollinate the knowledge within your frontline teams throughout different departments and levels of the organization.

One of the main reasons people leave your organization is directly related to issues with their manager. A Gallup study found that while 89 percent of employers believed their team members were leaving their company for more money, that was, in fact, accurate only 12 percent of the time. That same study showed that employees resigned 75 percent of the time because of issues with their managers.[28] Topping the list of their complaints?

1. A lack of direct communication with their manager, specifically feedback.
2. A lack of vision creating a feeling of being disconnected from the organization's purpose.

3. Being micro-managed and a complete lack of encouragement.
4. A lack of confidence in their managers' ability to lead them and the team to success.
5. A lack of empathy and a general sense their manager does not care about them or their career.

Consider these stats again and think about how many people at your company work for the middle leaders. Whether it's about appreciation, respect, dignity, or overall leadership skills, continually failing to invest in their training and development could spell turnover trouble, especially during this time of unprecedented resignations.

Let me put it another way. Suppose you invest zero time in training your middle leaders to be collaborative, supportive conduits of information who can liaise with ease both upward and downward in the organization. If that's the case, don't be surprised when your talented team members jump ship. Combine this with the knowledge gap among senior leaders regarding what is happening on the frontlines, and things will become tremendously risky. Making strategic decisions about the organization's future, both in products and people, is challenging enough; factor in a lack of clarity surrounding what is happening in the middle and at the frontlines of the organization, and you have a recipe for trouble.

CHAPTER THREE
REFLECTIVE QUESTIONS

1. Do the organization's senior leaders and executives spend time with the middle leaders? How do they hold them accountable for the experience they create for their teams?

   _____

   _____

   _____

2. Are the senior leaders listening carefully to the feedback they receive from middle leaders and the frontline team members? How is their feedback being actioned?

   _____

   _____

   _____

3. If investing in the leadership skills of the managers in the middle of the organization was a top priority, what would you do differently?

_____

_____

_____

4. How does your organization ensure information moves smoothly and accurately between the various levels within the organization?

_____

_____

_____

4

SENIOR LEADERS ARE OUT OF TOUCH

The higher up the ladder a leader climbs, the less
accurate his self-assessment is likely to be.
Daniel Goleman

We've all worked in organizations where the CEO, president, or executive team seems wildly out of touch with the other team members working closest to or at the frontlines of that same organization. The memos and all-company emails that appear ill-timed and out of place. New programs or tools that are launching when everyone is already working at full capacity, or how about the mandated full-time return to the office in a world where hybrid options are what employees really want? Actions like this make you wonder if anyone at the top of the organization is actually paying attention to what's happening.

Well, you're not crazy; the terminology for this phenomenon is *CEO disease*, which impacts many organizations worldwide.[29] This problem has become infinitely worse in the post-COVID world, where many organizations have transitioned into fully remote or hybrid work, and senior leaders have become further removed from their direct reports and the frontlines of their business. A recent study conducted by Workday of over 500,000 employees found that nearly one-fifth of them reported saying their leaders were out of touch with the stress they were feeling in this new post-COVID remote working world.[30]

The main challenge with CEO disease is the higher up the organizational ladder leaders go, the less feedback from the frontlines they directly receive. Instead, they interact primarily with other executives or senior leaders who likely have the same out-of-touch issue as them. It's like the game of telephone; the farther away from the message you get, the more distorted it becomes. When you consider the importance of accurate feedback when building or tweaking an organization's business plan or people plan, you can imagine how devastating this could be. It can also have negative impacts on the credibility of the entire executive team, who risk the appearance of being stuck in the ivory tower, not walking their walk, and inadvertently leading to a lack of buy-in across the organization.

CEO disease can also play a negative role in the further development and coaching of a team, whether that's an executive team, a middle leadership team, or a frontline team. If your senior leaders don't care to spend time with their people managers and their teams while executing their duties, how can they know firsthand where their strengths lie and what opportunities to develop they might have? How will they know what the experience is like for their people or their customers in a fully remote or hybrid world? The short answer is they won't. The result is the more senior the leader, the less likely they receive feedback or coaching. This lack of coaching also minimizes meaningful opportunities to collaborate, which can have several knock-on effects for the leader and their direct teams. It also sets a bad example about the importance of building a culture whereby leaders care enough to show up, give feedback, and create opportunities for worthwhile coaching and professional development. When these coaching activities aren't happening at the most senior levels of the organization, you're minimizing the likelihood they will occur in the middle of your organization, where they are likely needed most.

During my career, I've seen organizations where the leaders in some departments prioritized spending time in the trenches with their frontline teams. It created opportunities for those on the frontlines to engage with senior leaders in ways that helped them develop the skills needed to advance their careers. The "care factor" was evident in several of their coaching activities—for example, 360 performance reviews and job shadowing, which allowed for upward collaboration and feedback. There was ongoing coaching through development plans and weekly one-on-ones centered on what the team members needed to be successful. These coaching activities were happening diligently in some areas of the organization but not others. While it was a good experience for the team members in those specific departments, it also fueled an environment that created departmental silos where some team members were frustrated that these developmental activities were not taking place for them. I imagine it was a tough spot for those coaching leaders to be in. Do you continue to lead by example and create a coaching culture for your department, or do you follow the rest of the organization to ensure an equal employee experience? Not an easy decision. In that situation, my advice would always be to defer to those practices that can enhance the working culture for your direct reports. Make a difference in their lives and then try to influence other leaders up and down the organization. Be an agent for change.

Senior leaders can positively impact the workplace culture when they care enough to be involved with their teams, spend time on the frontlines, offer feedback, and provide coaching and clear direction. That culture will have many more positive impacts on the team members' overall life. Happy people tend to go home happy; they experience less stress and enjoy better overall health. Ground-breaking research from psychologist Anna Nyberg at the Karolina Institute in Sweden, a leading medical research university, found a direct correlation between destructive leadership practices and an increased risk of serious heart conditions in those she studied. She found when, among other traits, unclear direction, lack of feedback and encouragement, and minimal opportunities for leaders to listen to and collaborate with their employees were missing, this population had more heart attacks and poorer outcomes than those who revealed that these traits were present in their leaders.[31] Leaders who don't care are literally having a negative impact on people's health.

CEO disease in senior leadership teams can negatively impact workplace culture and people's overall mental and physical health, especially in a post-COVID, remote-working world. When senior leaders display indifference toward their teams, they are inadvertently grinding away at the foundation of a culture that enables their people to thrive in their current roles and develop new skills and abilities, readying them for their next career opportunity. Senior leaders and executives should take special care to find meaningful ways to connect with the organization's team members to ensure they have a positive working experience with their direct managers and peers.

CHAPTER FOUR
REFLECTIVE QUESTIONS

1. How do the organization's most senior leaders interact with the company's frontline team members? Do they solicit their feedback on the programs, systems, and tools they use?

   _____

   _____

   _____

2. How do your senior leaders measure the performance of the middle leaders? Do you know how they are held accountable?

   _____

   _____

   _____

3. What's the most significant change your executive team could make to enhance the development of the organization's leaders?

_____

_____

_____

4. How do leaders in your organization check in with their team members who work remotely? Does your company have mental health resources available should anyone need support?

_____

_____

_____

CHAPTER

5

EMPLOYEES FEEL UNDERVALUED

People work for money but go the extra mile
for recognition, praise, and rewards.
Dale Carnegie

The working world is suffering from an enormous deficit in appreciation. It's infuriating that something so easy to rectify seems to elude our workplaces. According to a recent study conducted by Gallup, one of the core drivers of employee turnover is, simply put, people don't feel appreciated.[32] Furthermore, in another study, when asked how the organization could improve engagement, almost 60 percent of those surveyed said, "By having more employee recognition."[33] Watching leaders worldwide spend time and money trying to figure out why their team members are leaving in droves

33

is perplexing. Study after study has shown that people leave when appreciation from the manager or the organization is missing. Inc.com, a leading periodical that advocates for small business and entrepreneurial success, found a staggering 79 percent of employees would leave their current roles because they do not feel appreciated by their manager.[34] It's not a complex idea to grasp; people want to be appreciated and recognized for their hard work, so why does this seem like such a foreign idea to some and challenging to execute?

It really shouldn't be a shock to us at this point to know team members want to be treated like human beings at work. Most people, by nature, want to be recognized and appreciated by their managers; it's a basic human need, after all.[35] They want to know that their work is valued and that they somehow contribute to their companies' goals. Interestingly, a study published by Workhuman, experts in humanizing the workplace, found that 73 percent of employees surveyed experienced less burnout and stress at work due to recognition. Additionally, 56 percent said being recognized made them less likely even to consider looking for another job, and another 44 percent reported frequent recognition made them feel like they were thriving in life.[36] Imagine that! Historically, the overall happiness of your team members has taken a back seat to the quest for enhanced bottom lines. However, recently, employee happiness has become a chief concern for senior leaders who are more than ever putting a greater importance on this crucial metric. A strong correlation exists between enhanced profitability and a happy, engaged workforce.[37]

One way to think about the importance of recognition and appreciation in your culture is to think about a concept brilliantly outlined by Don Clifton in his book, *How Full is your Bucket*. In his book, Don asks us to envision that each of us in the workplace carries around an invisible bucket, and each interaction we have with our colleagues and our leaders can do one of two things. Appreciation, kindness, and gratitude add to our buckets, filling them up, while criticism, negativity, or unkindness can drain our buckets, leaving us empty. The latter experience often leads to the team member feeling de-energized, depleted, and disengaged from the team and the organization, leading to their desire to leave. It's such a simple yet profound analogy. His book was given to me very early on in my leadership journey, and its simplicity significantly impacted me. To this day, I still recommend it to new leaders and those struggling to understand the implications of a culture lacking in appreciation.

It's essential to try and understand why some leaders are more prone to giving appreciation and recognition and why some are not. Part of the equation is generational in that the way some leaders view the idea of recognition and appreciation in the workplace varies significantly from others. Baby boomers, for example, required substantially less recognition than their younger generational cohorts.[38] A phenomenon like this is expected because of the world they worked in after World War II, where their leaders were more likely to use a command-and-control leadership style that grew out of the chain-of-command approach used in the military.[39] Considering Generation X has predominantly had the boomers as their leadership examples, you understand why the appreciation deficit has grown. Both Generation X and the boomer cohorts are misaligned, with the millennials and Generation Z now dominating the workplace, making up more than half of all workers today.

Millennials were raised differently than the Generation X cohort. They grew up in a time when everyone was labeled a winner, receiving ribbons for participation, and when kids received heaps of praise and recognition for even the smallest of accomplishments. Think for a moment about the implications of social media on this cohort. They were the first demographic exposed to the constant quest for likes, shares, and immediate gratification through social networking sites like Facebook and Instagram, which created a workforce that craves the same type of gratification from their managers and coworkers. Instant "likes" and "shares" of their jobs well done. And if this type of praise is missing from the workplace, the chance your younger team members will leave to go and find it elsewhere increases dramatically.[40]

Appreciation and recognition impact us in significant ways. When someone shows us appreciation or recognition, it reminds us who we are and what we have done has been seen by those around us and what we have done has proven valuable to someone. Being seen and providing value helps us build self-worth, something tremendously important in the quest to build self-confidence.

It makes sense then to consider how the opposite feelings would occur when appreciation is missing from the workplace as, unfortunately, in the world of hybrid or fully remote work, employees are often left feeling out of sight and out of mind from their leaders. They have feelings of being invisible, that no matter how hard they work, their manager and senior leaders simply don't see them or their contributions. Their hard work isn't valued because others don't see it. If people can't see how their work contributes to the overall organizational mission or objectives, it leaves them feeling disconnected and like their work doesn't matter.

The benefits to the organization of showing appreciation and recognition don't stop at the meaningful impacts on workplace culture and team members' morale. It can bring a sense of accomplishment, value, and connectivity to the more significant organizational goals while also shining a bright light on the behaviors and activities you want to see more of in your team. When you celebrate what *right* looks like where and when you see it, you illuminate a clear picture of what behaviors your team members need to display for them to be recognized and appreciated. In short, you see more and more of these behaviors happening across the entire organization because people want, at their cores, to feel valued and appreciated for their efforts. Think about how impactful this can be when working toward a series of business goals and objectives, especially since a lack of clarity is one of the main reasons people cite for not achieving their goals. More people can replicate those success-generating actions by shining a light on the specific activities that help advance us toward the goal.[41]

CHAPTER FIVE
REFLECTIVE QUESTIONS

1. When was the last time you were recognized for something you or your team accomplished? How did it make you feel?

_____

_____

_____

2. What would your senior leadership team do differently if recognition was a significant part of your organization's culture?

_____

_____

_____

3. How does your organization monitor appreciation levels among all team members? What prevents you from making appreciation a priority for your team?

_____

_____

_____

4. Is your organization comprised of more "bucket fillers" or "bucket drainers?" Who are the "bucket drainers," and what could be done to minimize their negative impact on team culture?

_____

_____

_____

6

A TOXIC WORKPLACE CULTURE

*Corporate culture is the only sustainable competitive advantage
that is completely within the control of the entrepreneur.*

David Cummings, co-founder of Pardot

The common thread that pulls all the parts of your organization together is culture, the experience people have when
working together for your company. It's a potent driver of
team engagement. A positive culture will earn the loyalty and
trust of your team members, while a toxic culture will earn
you the opposite: turnover and a poor employer reputation. A
study conducted by CultureX and MIT found, after analyzing
hundreds of companies and the sentiments of their employees
online, the number one driver of attrition during this great
resignation has been a toxic working culture.[42]

A toxic culture has a more significant impact on your organization than just attrition alone. Disengagement can run rampant throughout your departments and teams and has obvious implications for productivity, especially in a hybrid or fully remote working world. Additionally, internal and external relationships with key stakeholders can suffer, often decreasing innovation and creativity. A toxic culture can ultimately lead to the organization's demise when left unchecked for an extended period. So what leads to a toxic culture, and why is it so commonplace in today's working world? Research conducted by CultureX on over 1.3 million Glassdoor reviews found overwhelmingly, the most often cited driver of a company's overall rating is when employees feel disrespected, and it's most often indicative of toxic workplace cultures.[43]

Respect in the workplace is critical. Without respect, all the perks, fun events, and other parts of your total compensation become less valuable. When a robust social fabric exists, people treat each other with respect; it's a shared value and one that isn't easily undone or traded away for mere material compensation. Ensuring that your team members are consistently experiencing trust throughout the organization is priority number one and a good indicator of mutual respect between leadership and their teams. Suppose your team members indicate that trust is low within the organization. In that case, building the framework to rectify that sentiment as soon as possible is critical in mitigating further turnover and the disengagement of your best and brightest.

So how can you go about building a culture that's rooted in trust within the organization? Well, many behaviors and actions, when layered together and exhibited consistently over time, help you ladder up to trust. Harvard researcher Paul Zak, author of *Trust Factor: The Science of Creating High-Performance Companies*, suggests a people-first approach is the best path to creating a culture where trust prevails.[44] When leaders put the well-being of their people at center stage and spend time making sure they feel supported and appreciated and there are opportunities for growth and advancement, they put their trust in their leaders. And because trust between leaders and their followers is a two-way street, you, as the leader, must put trust in your team. Empowering them to take ownership of their work duties and projects is essential to that trust. Remember, you hired these individuals for their ability to do the job, so now it's time to get out of their way and let them shine. Conversely, micro-managing and diminishing your team's ability will destroy trust and disengage your people.

Now, empowerment and delegation are surefire ways to build trust and further develop your team. There is no doubt about that, but with this leadership style, there will also be errors and mistakes. It's inevitable that while you are encouraging your team to think for themselves and take the appropriate actions, sometimes they'll get it wrong. A tremendous opportunity for you to deepen your team's trust exists in these mistakes. Getting angry when they inevitably make a mistake will quickly erode trust. Instead, consider how you can turn that mistake into a coaching moment. Ask them to reflect on what happened and why things went wrong. Ask them what they might do differently in the future, and lastly, give them your perspective on what you might have done in that same situation. You will not only maintain trust, but it's an invaluable development opportunity. People learn differently; adults who learn through doing are prevalent in many workplaces, and they're bound to make a few mistakes.

Additionally, it's critical to understand how vital acknowledgment and appreciation are in building the foundation of trust in your company's culture and maintaining good interpersonal relationships. When you consciously acknowledge and appreciate your team members' accomplishments, not taking the credit as your own, it shows who you are as a leader and how you are trying to shine a light on your team's success. On the other hand, if you don't demonstrate appreciation for their efforts, you, as the leader, can appear selfish, like you're trying to take the credit. Selfishness is a quick path to the erosion of trust. Of course, a culture that uses appreciation and recognition significantly impacts the retention of your top talent and your ability to attract more like-minded individuals. A strong and healthy culture goes a long way in preventing talent attrition. Combined, you can see how a lack of appreciation, no career development, and poorly trained people leaders impact the overall culture your team experiences.

Building a culture of trust within your organization cannot be understated; it's that important. When team members trust you and their co-workers, wonderful things can happen. Team members are more likely to contribute their ideas and suggestions toward company goals and objectives, and they are more likely to be proactive instead of waiting to be told what to do. A high-trust dynamic leads to enhanced collaboration, a more substantial commitment to personal growth and development, and ultimately, far less attrition than companies with a low-trust working culture. It's vital to take an all-encompassing view of culture and what it takes to build one that is meaningful and rooted in shared values in the hybrid, remote, or in-person working world. Listen to what you hear in exit interviews about why people are resigning. A lack of advancement, limited professional development, and unappreciative leadership are signs of a toxic work culture. You will progress toward a more positive working culture by making meaningful enhancements in these areas.

CHAPTER SIX
REFLECTIVE QUESTIONS

1. How would you describe your organization's culture? How about your specific department or team? Is everyone living out the company's purpose and values?

   _____

   _____

   _____

2. What mechanisms are in place to measure the organization's culture? How do senior leaders share and action the feedback they receive related to culture?

   _____

   _____

   _____

3. In what ways does your organization put a people-first approach into its day-to-day actions? If people were their only priority, what would they do differently?

_____

_____

4. How much trust exists between the organizations' leaders and their teams?

_____

_____

_____

PART TWO

Closing the Culture Gap

The most powerful leadership tool you have is your own example.
Coach John Wooden

I spent my entire career, spanning twenty-five years, working for some of the world's most iconic brands. In each of those experiences, I had the opportunity to be onboarded, trained, and developed, and I worked alongside some truly remarkable leaders. I observed firsthand how these organizations managed communication, how the leaders made decisions, and how they rolled out system-wide initiatives to their frontlines and customers. I saw the good and the bad of multi-leveled leadership frameworks and lean structures with flat reporting lines. I worked in public and private companies and saw both their benefits and pitfalls. I attended countless conferences, training seminars, quarterly meetings, and corporate retreats. When thoroughly planned out, I saw how those events could benefit the business results and the organization's overall culture.

I also benefited greatly from two excellent tuition reimbursement programs: White Spot Restaurants and Starbucks. While also great for attracting millennials and Generation Z to your company, these programs helped me complete my first post-secondary education studies in leadership at the British Columbia Institute of Technology.[45] I also took advantage of two flexible work programs, one offered at Kelly Services and the other at Boston Pizza Restaurants. These programs offered me the flexibility I needed to complete a Master's Degree in Organizational Leadership from Royal Roads University.

While the work disruption caused by the COVID-19 pandemic certainly exacerbated the resignation problems many organizations face today, why people are resigning has plagued organizations for years. The following section addresses how to combat the great resignation and win the war for talent. It encompasses the best of the knowledge and tools I collected along my twenty-five-year journey to become the best leader I could be. I built these strategies from my experiences in the various organizations I worked for and my formal studies in leadership. I've learned over the years that leadership is like a backpack; you pick up many tools, philosophies, and ideas from all the leaders and companies you are exposed to over your career. I'm happy to share those with you in this next section to help you on your journey to create a winning workplace culture.

WINNING
CULTURE

PROMOTE
FROM WITHIN

MENTORSHIP

CONTINUOUS COACHING,
DEVELOPMENT AND
TRAINING

FREQUENT FEEEDBACK AND
PERFORMANCE ASSESSMENTS

ONGOING APPRECIATION AND
RECOGNITION

COMPREHENSIVE ONBOARDING AND
TRAINING PROGRAMS

HIRE FOR CULTURE FIT

LEADERSHIP ACCOUNTABILITY

7

A STRONG START

Coaching will become the model for leaders in the future . . . I am certain that leadership can be learned and that terrific coaches . . . facilitate learning.

Warren Bennis

A coaching culture begins on the employee's first day with the organization. You have but one chance to make a first impression, to set the stage and tone for how your new team members will assimilate into the culture and what they can expect from their leaders and co-workers. Consider the research from Tess Taylor, a contributing editor at HRDive, a leading periodical for human resource executives. She found 28 percent of people resigned from their positions within the first ninety days because of a lack of a formalized onboarding process.[46]

It's incredible that over a quarter of all new hires leave in the first ninety days because of a poor start. That alone is a good enough reason to ensure you plan for a robust onboarding and training experience to start on day one of your new team members' journeys. A robust onboarding experience can be delivered virtually or in person and can take on many forms with varied content, depending on your industry and specific needs. Still, every onboarding session should consider several common areas, regardless of industry.

A sound onboarding plan combines everything from the appropriate organizational protocols to your company's unique working culture and a million other little things sandwiched in between. It can be overwhelming, like drinking from the fire hose, so consider using a new team member handbook as your primary resource, having all your content organized and accessible after the fact is critical, as your new employee will likely have questions and need to reference the material later. Three specific "buckets" of information make onboarding go from good to great: People and Relationships, The Organizational "Why," and Training and Ongoing Support. Taking special care to ensure these buckets are well thought-out and well documented will help ensure things go smoothly on day one and your new team members feel set up to succeed.

People and Relationships

Perhaps the most critical part of any onboarding process is focusing on people and relationships; this is where the new employee starts to understand the culture and how it seeps into the organization's day-to-day work. Some of the best organizations in the world ensure each new hire meets with someone from the senior leadership team on their first day. Think about the statement this sends to your new employees; when a senior leader makes a point of sitting down with them, virtually or in person, to welcome them to the organization and share some words of inspiration, it's incredibly impactful. It's also a great time to remind them that each new hire has been hand-selected to join them on their mission to fulfill the company's purpose; it's a powerful statement. Also, consider adding smaller team meetings for this day so that your new teammates can not only meet others from the team but also start to see how the culture comes to life in the daily interactions of the group. Ensure you point out as frequently as you can throughout the day what the "good people practices" look like when you see them; this helps to paint a picture of what success looks like from a relationship perspective early on for your new hires.

The people section of your onboarding process should also introduce the importance of working partnerships, starting with their first partnership at their new company—their "training buddy." A buddy system in place on day one provides comfort to your new employees. Human nature tells us that most employees don't want to bug their new manager with what they may deem to be small or tedious questions. Getting that worry out of their head early on is important. So, introducing them to their go-to training buddy before their official training plan kicks off can help ensure that your new team members can dedicate more of their focus to important training content. When selecting the training buddy for your new team member, try to choose someone who is passionate, dedicated to the company, and can commit the appropriate amount of time to their new team member.

While tempting as it may be, do not abandon your new team members to a series of interdepartmental meet and greets on day one by themselves. These introductory meetings in the first few days are crucial to your new hire; this is where they learn what each department does to support the overall company objectives and their new role. By participating in the introductory meetings with your new team member, you have the opportunity post-meeting to check for understanding, ensuring they know who to go to for what. If time permits, it's a terrific idea to have your new team members spend a couple of hours with someone on the frontlines of each department later in their first or second week. This time, while an investment for sure, really helps to cement the knowledge of how each department works to support the organization's customers and frontlines. Displaying how the entire organization works toward shared goals can help to foster strong relationships and team building right out of the gate.

To help facilitate your new team members' ability to build strong relationships with their teammates, it's a good idea to ask them to schedule a thirty-minute one-on-one call with each of their direct team members to get to know them better. Providing some preliminary questions can help them break the ice and learn a little more about the team dynamics. Aside from the typical getting-to-know-you conversation, here are my top three favorite questions for introductory calls with new teammates:

1. What are you most proud of during your time working at [insert company name here]?

   This is a terrific question to start the conversation on a positive note, and it will give you some great information about their past team and individual successes.

2. What do you know now that you wish you had learned in your first few months at the organization?

   This is a great question to get essential topics, tools, or systems on their radar before their training begins.

3. What do I need to know about working for [insert manager's name here]?

   A great question to help them learn some details about the working style of their new manager, this one question can help your new team members get off to a strong start with that manager.

A final note on the people and relationship portion of the onboarding plan: try not to forget how overwhelming it is to start a new job at a new company. Remembering people's names, let alone who does what, is tremendously difficult. Providing a road map for your new hires for their first ninety days can be immensely helpful and give them one less thing to worry about. Remember, you want them to focus as much as possible on the most important content of their first days, so providing clarity on how and when they will get to know others in the organization can provide immediate relief. This road map should include, most of all, which relationships to prioritize and why. If you can, break it out weekly for the first three months: who to connect with, their role, their account-ability measures, and how their work supports the company's mission. Not only does this ensure your new team members continue building relationships across the organization, but they also learn how they can help them achieve their depart-mental and individual goals.

The Organizational "Why"

It's no secret that a strong organizational purpose embed-ded throughout the company is a core tool in the quest to retain and engage your workforce. Research conducted by leadership experts at the Dale Carnegie Institute found 83 percent of employees who identified as fully engaged be-lieved strongly in their organization's mission and goals.[47] The opposite was true for employees who identified as ac-tively disengaged. Furthermore, 88 percent of those actively engaged employees understood how their work tied into the organization's purpose. Being clear about your organization's purpose for your new team members and linking it to your mission and values right at the start can help them understand why their work matters in the early days of their employment with you.

An integral part of a robust onboarding process is how you, as a leader, immerse the new employee into the organization's mission. Doubling down on "success profiles" is a great way to ensure everyone in the origination knows what success looks like for each position in your organization, specifically in the hard-to-train soft skills. Success profiles are supplementary tools that accompany your training materials. They outline, by core competency, what an "A," "B," and "C" level of performance looks like. When used in week one as a part of your onboarding process, these tools ensure your new hires know specifically what top performance looks like in their role and how it contributes to the organization's success, taking all the guesswork out of the equation. It's important to reaffirm these success criteria frequently. When you give praise and recognition, big and small, in team settings or private, linking that recognition to the specific behaviors within the success profiles is a great affirmation.

Another vital tool in connecting your new employees to the organization's mission is to have clear, current, and well-documented operating procedures for each department. The operating procedures are invaluable for both new and existing team members. It's the link to the "why" things are the way they are and "how" those things, when executed to standard, impact your product, services, customer, or frontlines. Operating procedures also mitigate any gray area on how these procedures come to life. Lack of consistency is the enemy of achieving greatness, so the more tools and clarity you can provide your team members about what right looks like, the better their chance of achieving great results and enhancing your organization's success. These operating procedures will play several roles in your organization, not just as a tool for helping your new employees understand how their work links to the organization's purpose but also as invaluable training references, so keeping them up to date is crucial. Ensuring someone in your organization owns and updates these procedures as changes are made is a great best practice.

Training and Ongoing Support

Well-thought-out and consistently executed training plans are one of the most important things you can do to ensure your new team members' success and that they don't become a first ninety-day "turnover" statistic (see Appendix A and download your complimentary template at www.thegreatresignationtool-kit.com). Improper or lack of training is one of the leading reasons people leave their jobs in the very early days. Investing in proper training also helps to increase your organization's overall productivity in the long and short terms. Starting a new job, whether an internal or an external hire, is a significant growth experience and impacts productivity for the new team member and their team. Investing in comprehensive and consistent training programs helps to clarify the new hire's role and duties. Understanding their knowledge and experience gaps is foundational to tailoring their training needs in length and content to close them, ultimately helping your new team members get up to speed and build confidence much quicker. You likely already invest a significant amount of dollars in company-specific software, programs, systems, and tools, but failing to train your teams to use them effectively and efficiently means you could be wasting some of those initial investment dollars.

An important consideration when companies build their framework for training is understanding adults learn differently, so ensure you have methods to meet those styles. One sound method of training that incorporates different adult learning styles is the tried and tested Tell, Show, Do, and Review method.[48]

Tell

In this method, the "tell" is all about ensuring your employees know what tasks fall into their job description, their purpose, how they are executed, and how they contribute to the overall goals and objectives of the company. This stage of the training is vital for clarifying what the desired end state looks like and shines a light on some of the most common issues or problems that may arise when executing their role-specific tasks. This training portion is best done in person with a trainer, but recorded webinars, podcasts, and videos are also suitable. While verbal instruction is a good start, it is not enough to ensure a complete knowledge cascade for your new team member. Detailed job descriptions, success profiles, and standard operating procedures are good supplements to the "tell" portion of your training curriculum.

Show

In this method, the "show" is about the trainee observing the trainer completing the task themselves, from start to finish. Demonstrating the task for trainees is a perfect time to showcase what *right* looks like; completing the task to standard gives the trainee a good understanding of what the finished product needs to look like when they fly solo. A best practice is to have an organizational library of pre-recorded video demonstrations of the tasks so the trainees can go back later and review the trainer's work against their own. This added element of a video library for training purposes is essential to training younger generations like millennials and Generation Z. They've grown up with YouTube as a primary learning resource and the idea that you can show yourself how to do anything by watching and listening to videos online. At this stage of the training, it's also essential to identify if there are alternative ways to complete the task or if there is only one acceptable standardized method. Consistency is a battle many organizations face. Ensuring your new team members know the right and wrong ways for each function of their role will go a long way in achieving a more consistent finished product or service for your customers.

Do

The "do" step of this method is when the trainee gets to take everything they heard and watched and get their hands dirty! Allow plenty of time for the trainee to practice, and ensure you have activities lined up that will facilitate and enrich this practice time. The more you can ensure your practice activities mimic their real-world working environment, the more valuable the practice time will be. It's important to note that this is not yet what we call "solo practice time"; this time needs to be supervised by the trainer to provide ample opportunity for direct coaching, feedback, and correction. Remember during this portion of the training that while giving corrective feedback is indeed important, so is celebrating the things they get right. This appreciative approach to hands-on training will help your new team members build confidence and achieve maximum productivity faster.

Review

The "review" step is the final stage of the Tell, Show, Do, and Review method and is vitally important; unfortunately, it is often glazed over or missed entirely. How can your newest team members possibly know if they are doing well and on the right track if the trainer doesn't take the time to revisit the day's training session and review what went well and what needs additional focus? Timing is critical for this training element, and it's recommended the review happen immediately following the training activity while it's still fresh and top of mind. Completing the review the following day is risky. The more time that passes between the training activity and the review session, the more likely you will forget important coaching details, so build in time at the end of the session for the review.

Providing accurate feedback is vital and often requires conversational framing to ensure this discussion follows a specific path. Start with what the trainee did well during the hands-on session; this starts the conversation positively and lets the trainee know the areas of the activity in which they excelled. Next, focus on what didn't work so well, where there may have been issues with the process, execution, or timing; remember to be specific, and if you need to, refer to either the "tell" or "show" portion of the training once more. Finally, close the review with what the trainee should focus on to enhance specific areas of the task. Remember, training time is very different from practice time, and helping your trainees understand that will put them at ease. No one expects perfection on day one, so building adequate practice time into your onboarding and training timeline is important.

The final piece of the onboarding puzzle comes post-training, where two final tasks are important. First, once a new team member finishes their training curriculum, the official onboarding process is completed. Now is an excellent opportunity to gather feedback from them to understand, from their perspective, how the onboarding and training experience was. Ask them to rate the various elements of the program while providing anecdotal feedback on the individuals involved in their onboarding and training experience. Remember that new team members come to you with additional experience from different organizations and brands. Great companies know there is always room to enhance their programs, systems, and tools, and asking for your new hires' feedback is a great way to show them their opinions and ideas matter and are valuable to the organization. Secondly, ensure you have time scheduled in the calendars of the new team member and their manager to follow up on progress and assess for any gaps. Again, training is different from practice, and once the formal training wraps up, the practice begins. The buddy system is an essential element of this practice period. It's a great way to ensure your trainees feel supported in their role once the training program is complete.

CHAPTER SEVEN
REFLECT AND ACT

1. Think about the experience of your new team members on their first day on the job. What might their first impressions be? Could they describe the company's purpose?

    _____

    _____

    _____

2. How does your organization support trainees after their training period has ended? Do they know who they can go to for ongoing coaching and support?

    _____

    _____

    _____

3. Does your organization use specific training methods that support adult learning? How do you check for their understanding post-training?

_____

_____

_____

4. How would your daily leadership actions change if training became the most important focus for you and your team?

_____

_____

_____

CHAPTER

8

MANAGING PERFORMANCE AND DEVELOPING TALENT

The growth and development of people is
the highest calling of leadership.
Harvey S. Firestone

Now that your new hires have had a solid onboarding experience into your organization and robust training that set them up for success, the next step is to build a process for formally assessing how your team members perform in their roles throughout the year. Yes, the dreaded performance review. Don't stop reading now! It's essential to understand why most performance review systems go sideways, lack perceived value, and waste the time of your managers and your team members. Performance reviews, when poorly executed, contribute minimally toward an organizational culture built around coaching and skill-building. This next chapter will show how you can enhance the age-old performance review process to add tremendous value to the team members and the organization.

First, we need to talk about timing; I'm a fan of a formal annual review process because dedicating structured time to discuss each employee's performance at least once a year can be tremendously beneficial. This time can be used to celebrate their key successes and accomplishments, first and foremost, capping the year with formal appreciation and recognition. Second, you'll have an opportunity to discuss any gaps in their performance and build a plan to close them. For your top performers, this is a great time to discuss opportunities to develop new skills that could help advance their careers. But a performance review on its own, looked at only once a year, isn't going to yield many results. You need an all-encompassing process that lives on all year long. Don't fret; you don't need any expensive talent management software programs or expensive consultants to help you get this process off the ground. What is required is a commitment from you and your leadership team that talent development and performance assessments matter; once you have that, the rest is simply following the program.

A good performance development program has three core parts and can easily be delivered both virtually or in person: an annual 360 performance review, an action plan, and structured commitments around follow-up. We'll go through each element in detail.

The Performance Review

Most organizations' biggest mistake with their performance review process is using a one-sided, top-down approach. A process like this completely ignores the team members' perspectives and peer feedback from those who frequently work alongside them. This style of performance review process leaves a tremendous amount of room for manager bias to influence the appraisal of their team. I cannot overstate the implications of this review style, as it can significantly negatively impact the team member and their future promotability, financial compensation, and, ultimately, career success. If this is the style of review you are currently using, you would be better off not doing a performance review at all. Seriously.

A robust 360 performance review includes three core elements: the team members self-review feedback, feedback from a minimum of three stakeholders that the team member works with regularly, and the manager's feedback. Using the same questions to gather input from each stakeholder in the process is important. It will enable you to quickly triangulate the data from this process, ensuring that the team members' annual review includes only the core themes in their performance feedback. A simple *Stop*, *Start*, and *Continue* model is one of the most effective methods for gathering this feedback.

For example:

1. STOP: In her role as a regional manager, what could Sally "stop" doing tomorrow that doesn't add value to her relationships or the organization?

2. START: What could Sally "start" doing tomorrow in her role as a regional manager that would greatly benefit the organization and her working relationships?

3. CONTINUE: What areas does Sally excel in as a regional manager that she should "continue" doing in her role and perhaps share with other regional managers?

I prefer to work backward with these questions and start from the "continue" section as it tends to start the conversations off in a more positive and appreciative light.

Leading up to the performance review date, usually at least six weeks before you'd like to have the performance conversation with your employee, book time with three key stakeholders they engage with regularly. In the regional manager example above, you could connect with one of their regional manager peers, a general manager from one of the business units they support, and one person from a supporting department with whom they would commonly interact. Booking thirty-minute conversations with each stakeholder gives ample time to have the conversation. Having these discussions in person or via Teams, Zoom, Skype, or other video platforms allows for a much better dialogue and mitigates anyone's fears of having their feedback live forever in an email. You can align with your team members in advance of who you will speak to or select the people yourself and keep them confidential. Have a form with you (see Appendix B and download your complimentary template at www.thegreatresignationtoolkit.com) as you navigate each conversation and note the specific feedback in each bucket; you'll use this to triangulate the feedback once complete. It also makes an excellent reference tool during the action plan portion of the process.

At the six-week marker, you also send out the self-review form (see Appendix C and download your complimentary template at www.thegreatresignationtoolkit.com) and ask your team member to reflect on their performance throughout the year and completes the "stop, start, and continue" and send it back to you in advance of the performance discussion. The self-review is an excellent tool to help you gauge their self-awareness of any opportunities they may have to enhance their overall performance. As the manager, you also fill out the "stop, start, and continue" form, reflecting on the employee's year. As the manager, you will also factor the hard metrics into your review. For example, if your employee missed several key deadlines, you note this behavior in the "stop" section of the assessment. If the root cause of missed deadlines is poor planning, you would also note this behavior in the "stop" section of the review. The solution, better time management, for example, would be indicated in the "start" portion of the assessment.

As the manager, it's important to note that you mustn't rely on your memory alone at performance review time to capture your feedback; this often leads to a short-sighted review and misses core behaviors demonstrated throughout the year. A best practice I've used over the years and coached many others to use is to leverage a tool like Microsoft One Note for your ongoing observations and feedback throughout the year. After each one-on-one with your team members, open their file in

One Note and capture feedback linked to their preparedness, core issues or challenges raised, big wins, and any other relevant notes. I cannot stress how helpful these notebooks are when it comes to the annual review. You will have ample feedback and can easily see trends in that feedback, leading to reviews that are always rich with specific examples of the team members' behavior.

Once you've had all the discussions with your team members and their three key stakeholders, received their self-review, and completed your assessment, it's time to look at all the feedback, look for themes in the data, and write their review (see Appendix D and download your complimentary template at www.thegreatresignationtoolkit.com). If something is mentioned consistently by more than one stakeholder, it should make its way into the final employee assessment.

Another common mistake made when working through a performance review process is to have further coaching and development conversations simultaneously with the compensation discussion. These developmental conversations are critical, as it's the best time to discuss the root cause of any significant performance issues, and as such, you should never mix the two conversations. Best-in-class performance appraisals focus first on delivering the employee assessment and compensation decision. You then let the team member know that you will regroup with them in two to four weeks to discuss the next steps, which could include key areas for their ongoing development or any additional training required to close gaps. This approach gives the team members time to sit with the feedback and come prepared to discuss what's next from a development or training perspective, often helping avoid emotionally charged conversations. Giving corrective feedback is never easy, and the team member may not be in the right headspace to discuss further training or performance improvement needs now, so book the follow-up meeting and let some time pass.

The Action Planning Process

The rubber really hits the coaching road during the action planning meeting post-performance review with your team member. This meeting is usually an hour in length and has some prework involved, so when you send out the meeting request, ask the team member to come prepared to discuss the root cause of any issues flagged in the performance review and how they might work to close those gaps throughout the year. For your "A" players, the prework is a little different. Ask them to come prepared to discuss skills they would like to develop and their overall career planning goals. As the leader, you'll use one of three action plan templates to support the output of these conversations: Training Plan, Performance Improvement Plan, or Development Plan.

Training Plan

A new or updated Training Plan (see appendix E and download your complementary template at www.thegreatresignationtoolkit.com) is an excellent tool to use when you have uncovered gaps in the team members' knowledge or skills as a part of the review process. This is very common among your newest team members, especially in their first or second year with the organization. Given how much information cascades during the training process, it's almost impossible for them to remember and recall that information when it comes to applying it. Crafting a training plan to focus on areas of specific knowledge gaps is a terrific way to support the ongoing training of your team members. It also gives them additional confidence that their manager cares about their success and is willing to put the time and resources into further training to ensure their success. Training plans usually require a shorter time frame than a development plan that might run an entire year, but it depends on the number and significance of the gaps that need to be closed, so use your best judgment and air on the side of more time versus less.

Performance Improvement Plan

Performance Improvement Plans (see Appendix F and download your complimentary template at www.thegreatresignationtoolkit.com), or PIPS, as I like to call them, are often the most challenging for the manager to create and deliver to the team members because it means having difficult conversations about their overall performance or cultural fit for the organization. You must be brutally honest with the employee that their current level of performance is unacceptable and without meaningful improvements, their continued employment is not guaranteed. In my experience, while challenging, these are the most important conversations your managers will have with their team members. It helps keep "C" players in your organization to a minimum by being clear about expectations and gaps and putting the ball in their court. They have the choice at this juncture to own the feedback and work hard to change their course, or they can start to seek employment elsewhere, minimizing their risk of explaining a termination to their next potential employer. It's the most humane way to address significant performance issues, difficult for the manager but humane for the team members. Senior organizational leaders may have to lean in here with their more junior or less experienced people leaders and give them the tools and coaching they'll need to execute these conversations with their direct reports.

I firmly believe if you must terminate someone, it should seldom be a surprise for them. There should have been several conversations about the undesired behaviors and actions and what they need to do to enhance their performance and results. A Performance Improvement Plan identifies the critical areas of concern, the appropriate steps the employee needs to take, and a firm timeline for completion. A ninety-day timeline for these types of plans is usually sufficient. Remember to clarify for the team member what will happen at the ninety-day mark if their performance has not improved to the needed levels.

Development Plans

As a coaching leader, Development Plans (see Appendix G and download your complimentary template at www.thegreatres-ignationtoolkit.com) are the most enjoyable to build. Reserved for your team members who are meeting or exceeding all of the day-to-day requirements of their role, you now focus on developing new skills and abilities to help them prepare for a promotion or a lateral move. Identifying these team members through your review process is also crucial for building a bench of internal talent ready to be deployed elsewhere within the organization. Depending on the individual's needs, professional development skills are worthy areas to focus on during this time. You can help these team members work on core areas, such as public speaking, presentation skills, having difficult conversations, and cross-training within other departments to understand how other groups work to support the business goals. It could be the study of different leadership styles and when to use each for maximum impact; there are many possibilities depending on your industry, organization, and employee career goals. Many resources help in building these types of plans. I'm a big supporter of using books to develop talent; with minimal cost to the organization, books are a great way to expose your team members to different perspectives and expertise. I also like development sites like Coursera; again, with minimal costs to the organization, they can significantly impact your team's development. Visit www.thegreatresignationtoolkit.com to review my Leadership

Library, which lists some great resources you can use for your teams' development planning activities.

Following Up and Checking In

Once you have completed the action planning process for each team member, the most crucial part of creating a culture of coaching and development is the follow-up. There are two core elements of a good follow-up plan. First is the weekly one-on-one with each of your direct reports. It's a chance for you to observe and discuss weekly any links between their day-to-day work function and their coaching objectives in their training, development, or performance improvement plans. It helps keep these coaching conversations alive throughout the year. It is perhaps the most powerful tool you can use as a leader to ensure that performance coaching conversations are not a once-a-year event. A good one-on-one is team-member-led; the manager's role is purely for support purposes. This is not the time to review your laundry list of to-do items or cascade group information; use your weekly team meetings for this purpose. It's impressive how impactful a one-on-one can be when executed for the team members' benefit. Some research suggests that employees with regular one-on-ones with their managers are up to three times more engaged than those without.[49]

Arguably, the single most significant benefit of one-on-ones with your team members is simply checking in to see how they're doing. It's the least formal portion of the one-on-one but often the most valuable. Finding ways to connect with your team meaningfully and check in on their mental health and overall well-being is critically important, especially in this post-COVID world. Research conducted by the Kaiser Health Institute found that over 47 percent of Americans surveyed have suffered mental health issues since the beginning of COVID-19.[50] Regularly checking in with your team members shows them you care and can help align available resources should they need them. Ultimately, team members who are comfortable talking with their managers enjoy working at your organization more and are more likely to stay.

The next valuable follow-up tactic is to create a monthly development check-in, a designated opportunity for your team members working on development or training plans to spend time with you specifically related to their development or training plan progress. These meetings are invaluable; they demonstrate your commitment to their further learning and give them dedicated time to ask questions, check for understanding, and showcase their progress. It's important to note that this, too, is a team member-led meeting, and they create their agenda of items to review and questions to ask. It's an excellent time for them to share the key learnings from any developmental or training activities completed that month and highlight how they will apply their learnings to their work with tangible actions. It's also the time for them to highlight any areas they may be uncertain about or need to explore further, or how to apply the learnings to their role. You can act as a great sounding board or connect them with other leaders in the organization who may have more experience in the area they are working to develop.

A key message I have consistently delivered to my team members working on development plans to enhance their skills and abilities further is this work is always above and beyond their day-to-day duties, and sometimes *life* happens. Things get busy, and sometimes, no progress is made on their developmental activities that month, which is always fine! All I ever asked was they cancel that development check-in with a few days' notice so we could repurpose the time to more pressing issues and pick up again the following month. Setting this expectation right out of the gate relieves pressure on your team and helps them prioritize their workload more sustainably.

Prioritizing your team's ongoing coaching and development cannot be understated. The process may seem time-consuming, but the benefits are undeniable, and like most things, planning is vital. As outlined above, the entire process works out to seventy-one hours per year per team member. With a team of seven direct reports, the sweet spot, this equates to about 23 percent of your total work time per year.[51] Considering that a leader's number one job is to lead and develop their people, this is a small fraction of your time and time well spent.

Coaching Time per Team Member per Year

Weekly One-on-Ones x 50 Weeks	50 hours
Monthly Development Sessions x 12	12 hours
Annual Performance Review Process	9.0 hours
• Stakeholder Feedback Meetings x 3	2.50 hours
• Analyze Team Member Self-Review	.50 hours
• Analyze all Feedback for Themes	1 hour
• Write and Deliver Team Member Review	3 hours
• Build Development/Training/PIP	2 hours

CHAPTER EIGHT
REFLECT AND ACT

1. Think about your organization's performance review process. What could be enhanced or added to better support the coaching and development of your team members?

    _____

    _____

    _____

2. How many "C" players do you have on your team? What processes or tools exist to help manage them up or out of the organization? What impact are they having on your team's culture?

    _____

    _____

    _____

3. How do you currently uncover training gaps that exist with your team members? What tools or processes exist to help them to close those gaps?

_____

_____

_____

4. How do you currently identify the "A" players in your organization? What tools or processes exist to help further their development and career potential?

_____

_____

_____

9

COACHING LEADERSHIP

*The job of the leader today is not to create
followers; it's to create more leaders.*

Ralph Nader

Creating a coaching and development culture isn't simply
about a robust performance review process that includes development, training, and performance improvement plans.
That's what I like to call "table stakes." If you want to be the
best in class and attract the best talent in your industry, you
must do these things. It nurtures talent and creates a strong
pipeline of capable, intelligent, and driven individuals who
can effectively cross-pollinate ideas and skills across your
organization. Many other tactics can further your efforts to
develop and coach your team members. We will focus on what

I believe to be the most impactful for organizational health and bench strength: Inter-Departmental Teach-Outs, Formalized Mentorship Programs, and Impactful Feedback. Let's dive in!

Inter-Departmental Teach-Outs

Within any organization exists a wealth of knowledge and skills just waiting to be tapped into and shared broadly. A benefit of a robust performance review and development planning system is it helps senior leaders identify skills, knowledge, and abilities that exist within the company. This is the first step in sharing these skills and abilities more widely with all team members. One of the best ways to accomplish this cascade of knowledge is through a "teach-out culture." Teach-outs are easy to execute, spread the workload across many individuals, can be recorded for use in a development library, and fit perfectly in today's remote world.

Like most things, planning is key to solid execution, and this is no different. First, land on a teach-out format that works well for your organization. I used virtual meetings with a standardized presentation template and an agreed-upon framework for prework and post work. Generating the topics for knowledge cascades can fit nicely as a part of your annual departmental planning sessions or peopling meetings, which you'll hear more about a bit later. Topics can be agreed upon in advance and delegated to those best suited for creating that teach-out. For example, identify who in the organization excels at delivering in-person or virtual presentations, which is usually a top-cited developmental need, and enlist their support to build a teach-out that can be delivered to others in the organization. Have an in-house expert on handling objections and selling ideas? That's also a great skill to cascade down to others.

When applying this level of thinking, consider the skills that might exist across multiple departments. You'll see that there are likely many people in your organization who have something to offer in the development of others. As you start to deliver more and more of these teach-outs, surveying the entire organization for developmental topics that interest them is a great way to generate additional ideas.

These teach-out sessions usually last an hour to ninety minutes, are held monthly, and are scheduled at least a quarter in advance. They are always optional and can be layered into an employee's development plan if a good match exists between their developmental needs and the offered session. Prework is often a Ted Talk, a video, or a related podcast segment that serves as a good introduction to the subject matter so attendees come into the session with a basic understanding of the topic. The content of the teach-out is built by the presenter and reviewed by senior leadership for feedback and input. At the closing of the teach-out comes the post-work. Post-work exists solely to help cement learning and shouldn't be too lengthy or challenging to complete. For example, a teach-out I attended on hosting engaging virtual presentations included post-work that asked each attendee to record a five-minute mock presentation on a subject that inspired them and send it to their manager for feedback. Post-work like this is easy to execute and an excellent way to share your developmental activity with your direct manager.

Planning twelve months of teach-out sessions you can make available to all those in your organization isn't complex. Those who can attend on the scheduled day will, and by recording and cataloging these sessions, you build a repository of developmental topics, which individuals can revisit later. New team members can access them at their own pace during their training and onboarding time or later in their journey at the recommendation of their manager. These sessions also have the potential to become part of your organization's formalized training content for different departments and teams. These teach-out sessions are also a great way to expose team members from various departments to each other, break down silos, and increase interdepartmental collaboration—a win-win!

Formalized Mentorship Programs

It's no secret that mentorship programs can tremendously impact your team members' engagement and development. What might be a secret is how important mentorship is to millennials and Generation Z. A survey conducted by Deloitte found of millennials who said they would stay with their employers for more than five years, 68 percent of them had exposure to a mentorship program at work.[52] These are pretty compelling links to the retention of your top talent.

With traditional mentorship programs, it's not uncommon for those you select to serve as mentors within your organization to have seniority or senior experience gained throughout their careers, but also in other companies. Often, they serve or have served previously in leadership roles. That experience can significantly aid the development of future leaders in your organization, as mentees will have an opportunity to observe several different leadership styles in action. With the guidance and support of a great mentor, this exposure can help them progress faster through the ranks. At the same time, the person doing the mentoring often gains a much deeper satisfaction and purpose from their work; this can be immeasurably impactful and rewarding for the youngest boomers still in the workforce and the older Generation X now serving in senior leadership positions.

Another benefit of using mentorship programs to enhance your coaching and development culture is the bonds that can develop between people who may not otherwise interact between their departments. It creates opportunities for cross-functional collaboration that helps with silo-busting and enhancing existing programs, systems, and tools. By including the varying perspectives of your mentees in discussions with their mentors, you will inevitably learn things that may not have been visible to the mentor and those working in their department. Cross-functional relationships translate into well-rounded team members who understand how each part of the organization contributes to the company's success and develop new skills and expertise, another win-win!

There are several ways that you could go about implementing a formal mentorship program within your organization; the most common approaches are:

Group Mentoring—this is where one mentor has multiple mentees that require the same developmental expertise. Group mentoring is an excellent method to advance developmental opportunities and create interdepartmental relationships efficiently and is also a great fit for the remote and hybrid world. More silo-busting!

Peer Mentoring—this is where a mentor and mentee are on the same level within the organization. This type of mentorship is an excellent way to help close training gaps identified in the performance review process by pairing a mentor and a mentee from the same job role. Taking a mentor who excels in the area the mentee needs further training in allows for more practical learning through their experience and helps the mentor gain peer-to-peer leadership skills.

Supervisory Mentoring—this is the most traditional of mentoring methods, pairing a senior-level team member with a more junior team member. This type of mentorship is a terrific way to protect and cascade the human capital and knowledge within your older employees and advance the development of your future leaders.

Of course, as we discussed earlier, a solid mentorship program requires a commitment to planning to unlock strong execution. Consider including clearly defined goals for what you hope to achieve with your mentor-mentee relationships. Is the mentoring relationship mainly about transferring knowledge, developing leadership skills, or enhancing understanding of how other departments contribute to the overall objective? Whatever the goal is, ensure it is well-defined and that the mentor and mentee are aligned.

Next, you'll want to align on the process. Will it be monthly meetings, job shadow days, or informal connection time as needed? How you will measure success and the duration of the formal mentoring, keeping in mind this relationship will likely outlast the formal mentoring program. Ensure you give enough attention to matching your mentor and your mentee; a lot will hinge on the relationship they develop.

Well-developed and executed mentorship programs rarely take a one-size-fits-all approach. It could take several attempts at program design to get it right, based on your organization's needs and culture, and that's okay! It's more important to build a meaningful program, no matter how many iterations it may take, than to be too rigid when it comes to tweaking the program to get it right. Remember that allowing your team members to learn from others furthers their development and engagement and ultimately enhances your ability to retain top talent.

Impactful Feedback

When working toward a coaching and development culture, the final consideration, giving feedback, is perhaps the most important. We know it's beneficial to the employees, yet leaders often find it challenging to do this consistently. Giving feedback sounds easy, but most leaders, especially new ones, find it difficult to do. Perhaps this is why many employees suggest that it is almost non-existent in their working relationships with their managers. Why is this? Well, there is a good reason for this skill and practice gap. At our core, we all want to be liked, accepted, and respected and often fear we will jeopardize our relationships by giving corrective feedback.

I used to suffer from this affliction. My early years as a leader saw many instances of sweaty palms, sleepless nights, and anxiety leading up to difficult conversations involving corrective feedback. It was almost like I was having an allergic reaction to these types of discussions! It wasn't until I read *Tough Conversations* by Susan Scott that I began to see things differently. I began to understand that corrective feedback is an opportunity to help your employees grow professionally and enhance their skills and abilities when given the right way. And that withholding this feedback from them because it made me nervous and uncomfortable was jeopardizing their future career success. Giving feedback is a teachable skill, and like most things in life, the more you prepare and practice, the easier it gets. So what can you do to self-develop this critical skill? Four key focus areas exist in productive coaching conversations that require corrective feedback: intent, specificity, impact, and situational awareness. Let's discuss each in more detail.

Intent

The intent is the foundation for delivering corrective coaching that underpins how the employee will receive the message. The first thing you should always do when considering giving corrective feedback to one of your team members is to consider your intentions. If you intend to help the individual execute their role better or safer, you are starting from the right spot. When something goes sideways at work, sometimes the leader's immediate reaction can be to get angry or frustrated and look for someone or something to blame. When you react this way, your feedback lands more like punishment and can lead to defensiveness and tension, ultimately doing more harm than good to your working relationships. The intent is critical. Instead, take a moment to cool down and change your intention to come from a place of wanting to help others be more successful or perform their duties more safely. Doing so will help protect the relationships you've worked hard to build and turn missteps into coaching moments.

Specificity

Whenever you take the opportunity to deliver feedback to one of your team members, there are usually only two reasons you do so: to correct or change their behavior or to celebrate and maintain that behavior. In either of those scenarios, we must be specific when we deliver the message because failing to do so can leave them confused about what they need to change or what they need to continue. For example:

"Sally, your 'teach-out' today was a bit bumpy. Your slides were busy, so it was hard to decipher the key messages. You might want to remove some of the content so the message more clearly stands out. Also, your voice kept cutting in and out, making it difficult to understand. Did you test your technology beforehand? That's always a great way to see if things are running smoothly."

Conversely, "Sally, the teach-out you delivered today kind of missed the mark. You may want to practice a bit more before your next delivery."

See the difference? In one conversation, it is likely unclear to Sally what she needs to do differently, which doesn't allow her to learn and enhance her skills. In comparison, the other conversation leaves her with tangible takeaways she can incorporate the next time to enhance her performance. So be specific, very specific, and you will provide meaningful opportunities for your team to enhance and develop new skills.

Impact

An excellent way to think about specificity is to think of it as the content, the "what" of your feedback. Discussing the impact of that behavior or action is crucial to your team members understanding how that specific behavior impacts their peers, results, safety, culture, or the customer. They must understand how their behavior fits into the bigger picture and why it matters. It's arguably the most critical part of the entire feedback process. If you can't speak to how it's impacting a core area of the business or its performance, you may need to consider whether the feedback is worth giving. So make sure you take the time to consider the specific impacts of the behavior you are highlighting before entering into the corrective feedback conversation. The same is true when giving positive feedback. Your ability to tie the behavior back to how it impacts the overall business makes that feedback even more valuable to the team members. It increases the likelihood they will replicate the action in the future.

Situational Awareness

Last but certainly not least is your awareness of each situation or opportunity to give feedback. Situational awareness includes considerations, such as location, timing, your approach, and what else might be happening at that moment. With so many things to consider, this is the one area of giving feedback, specifically corrective feedback, that, when not properly executed, can negatively impact your organization's culture. No one wants to be given corrective feedback when they are upset, in front of their peers or customers, or when something else urgent or important is happening. You need to use your judgment when it comes to timing. Is the person in the right frame of mind to receive this feedback right now? Or is it better to wait an hour or until tomorrow or later in the day to have the conversation? It will be different in each situation, so properly considering the timing is critical. Just don't let too much time pass because the feedback can lose its impact when given too long after the situation occurs.

The final consideration regarding your situational awareness is an important one. You may need to consider that you might not have all the facts in the story; this is very common in personnel issues or customer/employee disputes. Remember that before the conversation takes place, you only have one side of the story, so it's best to ask for clarification and your team members' interpretation of events and ensure you have all the facts before proceeding. This additional step can save you from delivering unfounded corrective coaching that can ultimately deteriorate your trust and credibility as their leader.

Giving corrective feedback will likely never be easy for most leaders to do, and that, from my perspective, is a good thing. When you get a little bit nervous leading up to these conversations, it shows you are giving the discussion the consideration it deserves and you care about your relationship with your team; that's why you want the conversation to go well. Follow this formula and practice. With each conversation you have, you'll enhance your skills, and remember, you are having a significant impact on the development of your team, ultimately helping them enhance their performance.

Creating a culture of coaching and development takes commitment from all the leaders in your organization, a commitment to sharing knowledge broadly across the company in a structured way. A commitment to connecting mentors and mentees in meaningful ways will impact your team by creating opportunities for them to learn from those with specific knowledge to share. And finally, a commitment to enhancing the feedback delivery skills of your people leaders. Ensure the feedback they give is specific to the behavior in question, linked to the behavior's impact on others or a business result, and delivered with good intent and in a way appropriate for the situation. Committing to the growth of the talent in your organization in this way will go a long way to helping you build and maintain a culture of coaching and development that engages, retains, and attracts top talent to your organization.

CHAPTER NINE
REFLECT AND ACT

1. Thinking about your current team, department, or organization, who has specific skills or abilities that could be shared more broadly to benefit the entire team?

    _____

    _____

    _____

2. When was the last time you received feedback from your manager? How was it delivered? How did it make you feel?

    _____

    _____

    _____

3. When was the last time you delivered feedback to one of your team members? How did the conversation go? How did they react to the feedback?

_____

_____

_____

4. Does your organization have a formal mentorship program? Who do you know that could benefit from having a mentor?

_____

_____

_____

10

APPRECIATIVE LEADERSHIP

People work for money but go the extra mile
for recognition, praise, and rewards.
Dale Carnegie

When it comes to how recognition makes people feel, there is little doubt it has a tremendous impact on our well-being and how engaged we are in our workplace. Sadly, a lack of appreciation and recognition has become one of the top drivers of turnover and why people seek employment elsewhere. A study conducted in 2020 by Energage, a leader in workplace culture research, found appreciation was the top driver of employee retention, keeping people deeply connected to their work.[53] Similarly, research conducted by Gallup in 2021 found teams who regularly received praise and appreciation for their efforts felt the work they were doing was incredibly valuable to the organization's purpose.[54] So if you are trying to close your culture gap, an evaluation of your current levels of team member recognition and what programs exist to support your leaders in celebrating their top talent deserves to be at the top of your list. Appreciation has four significant impacts on your organization: enhanced trust in leadership, team satisfaction, humanizing your people, and a positive culture.

Enhanced Trust in Leadership

Trust in all levels of leadership is a foundational element of how your team members experience life at your organization. Creating an environment where trust can flourish can be difficult when an ever-increasing number of employees work remotely and in-person, one-on-one time with their direct manager becomes scarce. One way to increase trust is to show that you value and appreciate your team member's contribution to the overall organizational goals and culture. So it is crucial to take the time to shine a light on the positive contributions your team members make, especially when you do it in a way that highlights the specificity and the impact of the action. It shows them you are paying attention to their work and want to celebrate them and their accomplishments when things go well. Confident leaders always spotlight their teams' great results; this ultimately displays your commitment to them and their success, which builds their trust in you as their leader.

Team Satisfaction

When someone recognizes your efforts, it just plain old feels good. It can put a smile on your face and make you feel more secure in your overall performance, which can have a chain reaction throughout the rest of the team, the department, or the entire organization. People typically want to work in environments where their peers are positive, energized, and a little more cheerful. It's contagious. Conversely, the same could be said about the opposite. If you have to go to work every day with negative people, it tends to suck the energy out of the team, which can lead to widespread disengagement, the kiss of death for any company culture. When people are happier and more secure, they also tend to have higher degrees of confidence, which can impact their overall productivity and performance. Many senior leaders now recognize that the happiness of their employees directly impacts the bottom line. As a result, they are putting more of their efforts into this area. It just makes good business sense and human sense. Another win-win!

Humanizing Your People

It shouldn't come as a surprise to anyone that your team members want and expect to be treated by their managers and their organization as human beings, not as numbers on their payroll. I call this the "be a good human factor." Treating people with respect and dignity should be commonplace in all workplaces, as should showing appreciation for a job well done. After all, feeling recognized and appreciated is a basic human need. When someone takes the time and makes an effort to highlight our achievements and contributions, it makes us feel proud of our work, which can offer us a greater sense of meaning and accomplishment, a sense that we are contributing to a more significant organizational purpose, something bigger than our individual contributions. Once again, it's essential to be specific about the behavior you highlight and its impact on the overall business. Specificity shines a light on the right behaviors and actions and ultimately shows others on the team what right looks like; this often leads to more of that behavior displayed across the organization.

Being a good human also means taking care of your team members when and where they need it. Life can be difficult for everyone at one point or another, especially in this post-COVID world. Mental health issues, especially among the younger generations, are at an all-time high compared to what they were only a few short years ago.[55] While no one expects leaders today to also act as qualified mental health professionals, being on the lookout for signs of trouble is the right thing to do. By checking in with your team members frequently and being aware of sudden changes in behavior and attitude, you can quickly, if needed, put them in touch with the right kind of support. It's also a good reminder to have a strong situational awareness when delivering difficult coaching and feedback. As best you can, ensure they are in the right frame of mind to receive this coaching. Remember, leaders exist to serve their people in whatever way makes the most sense for each individual on their team.

Positive Working Culture

Last but certainly not least is the impact recognition and appreciation have on your working culture, which is critical because a toxic culture is one of the main reasons people leave their jobs. Conversely, a positive and healthy working culture can be the main differentiator in how your company attracts and retains the best talent in your industry. The best cultures always put people first. They have leaders who shine a light on their team members and their accomplishments, build trust, and treat their people as human beings with respect and dignity. Senior leaders focus on the overall happiness of their departments and teams by ensuring they have a culture built on consistent appreciation and recognition, not only by their leaders but also from peer to peer. If you follow in these leaders' footsteps, you will be well on your way to creating a culture of which people want to be a part.

Now that we understand the benefits of investing in developing a culture of appreciation and recognition, let's discuss how to accomplish this vital leadership task. There are two main strategies for building the framework that can help unlock consistent appreciation across the organization: formal and informal recognition programs. A formal recognition program is executed equally and consistently across all departments of the organization and tends to happen at specific times throughout the year. Informal recognition programs are tactics not bound by recurring dates and themes, giving leaders and their teams flexibility on what gets recognized and when. Both strategies are integral to ensuring this type of culture, where people feel appreciated and recognized, can thrive throughout the organization and have a meaningful impact on all.

Formal recognition programs often include celebrating your team members' birthdays, length of service awards, marriages, adoptions and births, and other significant milestones that can happen throughout one's life. There are no limits to what you can celebrate here. The primary concern is to ensure it is celebrated equally across the entire organization; otherwise, celebrating some team members' significant life milestones and not others can do more harm than good. Favoritism does not enhance your workplace culture; it detracts from it. So align with your senior leaders on those milestones, and then go forth and celebrate!

These types of celebrations don't have to be costly. In my experience, one of the most valuable things a manager can do to celebrate these events is the simple act of a handwritten card, which has such a personal touch and never goes out of style. When it comes to the length of service awards, there are many companies that can manage these programs on your behalf. However, as a recipient of many of these autogenerated cards and emails, I will say that nothing trumped a handwritten card from my manager. Monthly department team meetings or organization-wide meetings are another way to shine a light on these significant milestones. However, a word of caution: before celebrating in public, it's a good leadership practice to check in with your team members on how they like to receive recognition, in public or private. Some people are a little more low-key than others, and taking that extra step to check in with them on this subject is another little way to show them you care and want the experience of being recognized to be meaningful for them.

An annual awards program based on departmental and organizational results is another formal recognition program that can hugely impact the organization's overall performance and celebrate your top achievers. Several companies I've worked for have gone all out to celebrate these types of awards in a big way, either at year-end holiday parties, annual conferences, or annual award galas. The programs are hugely impactful and can spark just the right amount of competitive camaraderie within the organization. There is no limit to what these awards categories can be, but here are some very common practices:

- **Customer Satisfaction Awards** celebrate people or teams their clients or customers have frequently recognized for exceeding their expectations.
- **Sales Attainment Awards** are typical in sales-based organizations and are awarded to those who meet or exceed their sales targets annually or by quarter.
- **Team Player Awards** can be some of the most impactful awards to give out each year as they are often peer-nominated. They spotlight your team members who always put the team first and do everything they can to help others succeed. What better behavior to shine a light on in your organization!
- **Leadership Awards** are a terrific way to recognize your leaders who significantly impact the company's overall values and culture. When building a culture of

development, coaching, and appreciation, think about linking your leadership awards to these behaviors. Celebrate those who walk their talk!

*   **Rookie of the Year** is my favorite type of award as it allows the celebration of some of your newest team members who have made an immediate impact in your organization. Often, team members who have not been with you the entire year aren't included in these annual award programs, so this is a great way to celebrate those rock-star new hires with a category all their own!

Another impactful formalized recognition program is implementing a "Team Member of the Month (or Quarter)" Award. These types of recognition programs allow for more frequent awards to be handed out within the organization or department and create more formal opportunities to celebrate the achievements of your shining stars. The most effective and impactful programs I have seen or been a part of have always been peer-nominated, as it takes away any opportunity for manager bias to creep in. Additionally, being nominated and celebrated by your peers for always going above and beyond feels excellent. Again, these annual or quarterly awards don't have to be costly to implement. In my experience, formalizing these programs with a plaque, a handwritten card, and perhaps a small token of appreciation is all it takes to make the team member feel the love; no new car required!

While these formal programs contribute in strong and meaningful ways to a culture rooted in appreciation and recognition, the informal strategies show your team members daily that you appreciate all their hard work and bring the culture to life. Starbucks was one of the best organizations I worked for in this regard. Shining a light on team members' success was second nature in every Starbucks leader I worked with. Their actions helped show me as a leader in the organization how I, too, could contribute to this culture, embedding recognition and appreciation in my day-to-day role. Some of the best tactics that made an impression on me and that I took with me on my leadership journey were the following:

- **Meetings**—at Starbucks, the start of every meeting, no matter the purpose, always includes two things: a coffee tasting and recognition. The coffee tasting signified the importance of coffee to their culture, and recognition started the meeting off in a positive light and put their people first. The recognition could be as simple as celebrating positive feedback from a customer, a recently completed project, or someone who went above and beyond to help another team member or department. Whatever the reason and without fail, every meeting started in this way.

- **Caught Doing It Right**—Starbucks does an incredible job of being very clear about what behaviors are fundamental to their culture. They call these the "Green Apron Behaviors": being genuine, welcoming, knowledgeable, considerate, and involved. They have clear descriptions of each behavior, and every time you experience a peer going above or beyond in one of these areas, you could give them a Green Apron Card that thanks them and celebrates them for their actions. It created a positive atmosphere in the head office and the stores, with peers celebrating peers!

- **The Good Human Factor**—above all else, it was my experience that the people who worked at Starbucks displayed the "good human factor." They went out of their way to appreciate the big and the small things people did for each other, and that appreciation went such a long way. I've never worked with so many "servant leaders," people who went out of their way to help you or the business succeed. Having had the opportunity to spend time with Howard Shultz and Howard Behar, this is unsurprising. They both believe at their core that leaders exist to serve their people and their communities, and seeing that come to life in an organization is incredibly inspiring and engaging.

While Starbucks is a massive organization with thousands upon thousands of team members worldwide and many resources at its disposal, it doesn't mean these ideas won't also work for your organization. What behaviors mean the most to you and your company? Do your team members know that these behaviors matter? How do you set the tone at the start of your meetings? Do you take time to shine a light on what's going well, or do you dive right into the agenda for the day? Do you remember to thank people for the small things? Do you ask your team members how you can help them? What might you do to make things go a bit easier or smoother for them? These actions cost little to no money to implement yet can have a tremendous impact on how your culture of appreciation and recognition comes to life day in and day out.

CHAPTER TEN
REFLECT AND ACT

1. How does your organization monitor and measure trust between its leaders and their direct reports? Is your organizational culture built on trust?

    _____

    _____

    _____

2. What formal recognition programs are currently used in your organization to celebrate top performers? What could be added or enhanced in these programs?

    _____

    _____

    _____

3. What else could your organization's leadership teams do to put their people first? How do their team members know they care about them and their well-being?

_____

_____

_____

4. What little behaviors exist in your organization or department that let your team members know their efforts are seen and appreciated?

_____

_____

_____

11

LEADERSHIP ACCOUNTABILITY

Accountability is the glue that ties commitment to the result.

Bob Proctor

Great organizations know commitment without accountability often leads to great plans and ideas with little traction or concrete results. Creating a culture of coaching, development, and recognition is no different. You must install checks and balances along the way to ensure the values and commitments expressed at the company's top filter down to those working on the frontline. Without this level of accountability, your probability of achieving sustained success is limited. Accountability starts at the top; it starts with you.

Many tools and processes can help to ensure that things like 360 Performance Reviews and the ensuing action plans are happening throughout the organization. From robust technology solutions like a human resource information system (HRIS) to having the processes live internally with HR or senior leaders, choosing the right approach depends on your organization's size, budget, and available people resources to manage the process. It doesn't have to be complicated, time-consuming, or costly to ensure your leaders execute meaningful reviews and development plans. It can be as simple as each senior leader meeting with their people managers to review each of their team members' assessments and their recommendations for the next steps. Senior leadership can spark new ideas that enhance the development plans or training plans that your team members require, and this final check-in is often all it takes to ensure this process is done and done well.

Peopling Meetings

Another effective tactic to ensure the exposure of top talent and the management of poor performance happens across the senior leadership team is to host quarterly talent review meetings, or "peopling meetings," as I like to call them. Each quarter, you get the senior leaders from across the organization together for a one-day meeting to discuss the upcoming people needs within each department and any internal candidates that might exist across the organization who may be suitable for the role. A forum like this creates a great line of sight for leaders while they're considering their people resource needs for the upcoming year. During this meeting, reviewing any

"C" players you may have in your department and the expected outcome is critical. This discussion is integral to the people planning process as any anticipated gaps become evident across the organization. You can discuss how best to fill that gap and if you have someone internal ready to step into that role or if you will have to hire from outside because you don't have the available talent. Peopling meetings are essential for any organization that wishes to have a "promote from within" culture. Senior leaders must present their top and bottom performers with the accompanying plans to support both groups.

Peopling meetings are also great venues to review the plan for your monthly teach-out sessions. Since you'll be discussing, department by department, your top talent and their developmental needs, you can assess the organizational themes in developmental areas and link those back to potential teach-outs and who in the organization is best suited to deliver them. You can create a learning and development calendar up to three months before these sessions begin by conducting your peopling meetings quarterly. Doing so ensures adequate time is given to those preparing the session and plenty of advance notice to those who wish to attend the session. Peopling meetings are also an excellent time to discuss potential mentoring opportunities that might benefit the organization's top talent and match them with the appropriate mentor. You'll have all the right people present to generate the necessary approvals, speeding the process along.

Performance review debriefs between senior leaders and their people managers and specific peopling meetings are solid tactics to ensure your review process is happening effectively across all levels of the organization. It also gives you time to plan for your top talent's developmental teach-out and mentorship needs. However, ensuring consistent coaching, feedback, and recognition are executed consistently within your departments requires additional accountability measures. In my experience, three tactics can help create that extra layer of accountability: an annual all-team member culture survey, stay interviews, and yearly departmental skip levels.

Culture Surveys

At this point, we understand the significant impact your organizational culture has on your ability to attract and retain top talent and on the overall engagement of your workforce. So it would make sense that measuring the health of your culture at least once per year could yield terrific insights into where you are doing well and where you may have some more work to do. Consider using a tool like SurveyMonkey to assist you in building a culture survey focused on your organization's cultural goals and values. You can create specific questions related to a culture of coaching and appreciation, things like the annual performance review process and the action plan that follows, and the quality and frequency of feedback and recognition the team members receive.

Measuring the health of the relationship between your leaders and their team members and their connection to the company's purpose will give you sound benchmarking data. These questions will allow the organization's senior leadership team to truly understand how their employees are feeling and themes that may be showing up in the data. It will also help the senior leaders get ahead of any issues that may be brewing within a specific team or department. It's a good idea to ensure these surveys are anonymous and only provide links to the business unit or department. For your team members to have confidence they can answer openly and honestly in this survey, their anonymity is essential. I've included some sample culture-related survey questions (see Appendix H and download your complimentary template at www.thegreatresignationtoolkit.com) to help you get going!

Of course, a survey like this is only as good as the action taken as a result, so the transparency of results and any subsequent action is necessary. Two specific tactics can be helpful here. First, holding an organization-wide team meeting or sending out an all-team communication post-survey allows the senior team to celebrate the great things people have said about the organization's culture. It also creates an opportunity to shine a light on areas where the organization can improve and the immediate and long-term plans to close any gaps. Next comes department-specific meetings where the department leader can highlight their specific culture-related wins and areas where additional work is needed to close any gaps. As with any good action plan, involving your team members in generating ideas to close those gaps often leads to a more robust and inclusive action plan that everyone buys into. Benchmarking your results yearly provides the necessary tool to measure your progress and track the areas that are improving and those that still need work. Remember, what gets measured gets fixed!

Skip Levels

Skip levels, simply put, are meetings where the senior leader meets with the direct reports of the people managers under them. They are essential because they help bridge the gap between the senior leadership team and those working several levels below them. They can also play a vital role in the ongoing development of your leadership teams. They are a tool for accountability and commitment to the organization's goals around creating a coaching, development, and recognition culture. Skip-level meetings are one of the main tools an organization can use to help keep a pulse on how the team members feel. You'll also gain insights into the culture and the working environment through direct conversations with people you couldn't get any other way.

The main objective of a skip-level meeting is to enhance the communication and flow of information within your organization. When you want to assess how well the various teams understand the goals of a department or the company, skip levels provide the venue to get a sense of how managers relay information to their teams. It's also one of the best venues to get developmental feedback for your leaders. Often, the higher up the organization leaders go, the less feedback they receive about their leadership practice. In authentic learning organizations, leaders at all levels of the organization continually work on their leadership craft. Another often understated value that comes from skip-level meetings is they can be used to personally demonstrate how you, as a senior leader, value team members' feedback at all levels of the organization. It's another one of those rare ways to walk the talk of "everyone's opinion matters" and ensure it's just not some catchy slogan on the board room wall. I've included some potential skip-level questions (see Appendix I and download your complimentary template at www.thegreatresignationtoolkit.com) to help you get started on your accountability journey!

Again, like most mechanisms for feedback, they are only as good as what you do with the information. Action planning and follow-up are critical here too. You will undoubtedly hear positive feedback about the leader and how they engage with their teams; celebrate this feedback with the manager. We already know how appreciation and recognition can positively impact your team, so make a point of debriefing with them post-skip level. You may also be made aware of some dysfunction within the team or department; this is an opportunity for you to provide detailed feedback and coaching to the manager and discuss ways to change course or enhance that specific area of their leadership practice. Remember, feedback is crucial to creating a culture of coaching and development.

Stay Interviews

The final tactic we'll discuss to help you on your leadership accountability journey is a tool widely underused in organizations today: stay interviews. Like the standard exit interview used after one of your team members resigns, the stay interview (see Appendix J and download your complimentary template at www.thegreatresignationtoolkit.com) is meant to stop top performers from leaving in the first place.[56] They are an excellent leadership practice to understand how your team members are experiencing life in your organization, specifically, the areas that may be causing them frustration or dissatisfaction in time for you to do something about it. A good best practice is to start at the top of your team roster and work through that list quarter by quarter so you have had a stay interview with all your core team members by the end of the year. And not wanting to sound like a broken record, the feedback you receive during these interviews needs to be acted upon. Otherwise, your team will quickly see there is little point in them sharing their experience with you if nothing is done to correct any of their concerns.

It's important to understand that a culture of accountability starts at the organization's top with the president and senior leadership team. To truly understand how the frontlines are experiencing the company's products, systems, or tools, they must go to the frontline and observe them for themselves. Walk the factory floor, so to speak. However uncomfortable this may be at first, the feedback they will receive and the trust they will build with the frontline team members will be invaluable. Often, the people who use these systems and tools created by more senior levels of the organization have the most impactful feedback that can help enhance those tools further, things you could only know if you used them daily. By missing this opportunity to interact with the frontlines, you will fail to gain these important insights and miss another chance to walk the leadership walk. While you may not be an expert in the work on the frontlines, I guarantee you will learn ways to make life easier for your team. You'll understand how to enhance the tools and systems that will generate a better product, deepen relationships across all levels of the organization, and have some fun in the process.

CHAPTER ELEVEN
REFLECT AND ACT

1. How does your organization currently ensure a culture of accountability exists with its leadership teams? What is missing or could be enhanced?

   _____

   _____

   _____

2. Do you know what frustrations might exist with your top performers and could lead them away from your organization? What is preventing you from finding out?

   _____

   _____

   _____

3. Do you know why your recent resignations left the organization? Was anything done to act upon their feedback to mitigate that experience for others?

    _____

    _____

    _____

4. Do the leaders in your organization walk their talk? Do they do the things they say they will do? How does this impact a culture of accountability?

    _____

    _____

    _____

12

CHANGE LEADERSHIP

Leadership deals with people and their dynamics,
which are continually changing. The challenge of
leadership is to create change and facilitate growth.
John C. Maxwell

Many people and organizations have the will and the desire to change, but let's face it, change is hard. Very hard. Often, the will alone is not enough to create or sustain change in the long run. Change initiatives fail for many well-known reasons: lack of planning, vision, misalignment of the organization's values, or a lack of resources. But one of the main reasons change fails is the reason that gets the least attention and has limited organizational awareness, "change fatigue."

In today's ever-changing landscape, people are tired, and in the post-COVID world, where everything looks and feels a bit different, your team's ability to cope with change is about 50 percent less than what it was only two short years ago.[57] Whether it's their work location, expanded workload, or new policies and procedures that take time to adjust, people are experiencing significant levels of change fatigue. So how can we acknowledge this issue within our organizations yet continue working toward building and sustaining a culture of coaching and appreciative leadership? Well, two main tactics can help mitigate the fatigue of constant change: identifying and celebrating all the early successes of the desired change and creating team member and leadership experiences connected to the vision for change.

Celebrate Early Wins

Celebrating early wins is a great way to feign off change fatigue and a hallmark of the appreciative leader. Shining a light on what is going well as it relates to the change vision helps the team members see their new behaviors are a part of the desired change, and we already know recognition feels great and drives engagement and retention, a win-win. For example, seeking out leaders who do a great job with the new performance review process and celebrating them will help cement this new behavior. Similarly, looking for those team members who go out of their way to appreciate their team or their peers for a job well done, pitching in a lending hand, or any other recognizable effort is something else worth celebrating. When you shine a light on what *right* looks like, you often see more of that behavior throughout the organization. It's important to start looking for these wins early; often, it's the most critical phase of your change management plan.

Whenever you embark on a large-scale change management initiative, especially something as important as culture, you must remember that change is hard for people even in the best of times. A strange place exists between the time when a team member knows the old behaviors and ways of doing things are no longer the norms, but the new ways of doing things are not yet permanent parts of the culture. This place is called "no man's land."[58] The place where the old ways are in the past but the new ways are not always clear and don't yet feel comfortable. During this phase of change, you need your leaders to be in the trenches with their team, shining a light on the pathway forward and what right looks like. It's a tricky spot for people to be in. You go from feeling secure and confident in how you do your job one day to a new awkward place where you are uncertain if you are even meeting basic expectations. Constant and consistent recognition of the right behaviors is the antidote for no man's land, but you must be side by side, working with your team to "catch them doing it right."

"Backsliding" is one of the risks associated with the early stages of change; it's when the team members stuck in no man's land feel such uncertainty that they revert to the old ways of doing things. Backsliding is most common when leadership is not in the trenches with their team, modeling the way. It may feel like you are micromanaging during this stage, but it is crucial to fight off the urge to pull back and stay close to your team; feedback is vital at this stage. Celebrate the right behaviors and remember that your other main priority during this stage is to act as a role model for the desired behavior. Ensure you give feedback often and that your intent for this feedback is for their further learning and development. Be specific, highlight the impact of the behavior or action, and always remember your situational awareness. The same is true for giving positive feedback, especially the specificity and the intent. Highlight the exact behavior and why it's so important.

Experience the Change

Creating opportunities for your team members and their leaders to experience the new systems, tools, and processes together can help alleviate uncertainty and serve as a time to bond with each other as you all work to find your way. Considering what these events might be and then communicating them numerous times to those impacted is a crucial part of building your overall change plan; doing so helps to belay some of their fears of the unknown. Plan, communicate, follow up, plan, and communicate some more. It simply cannot be overstated the importance of clear and frequent communication throughout the change process.

When contemplating how you might roll out something like your new 360 Performance Review process, consider hosting several "lunch and learn"-style training sessions. One set of sessions for the leaders who will be using these new tools and techniques and then one set of sessions for their team members. This advanced exposure enables lots of time to review the new program and engage in Q&A for any areas that make them feel uncertain. Set a clear timeline for when the new review process will start and exactly how it will work. Remember, the goal here is to expose people to the new tools, review them at the most comfortable time, and then provide clear direction on who they can go to with questions or concerns. These sessions are well worth the time and effort they take to execute. They could also be considered for teaching leaders how to give effective feedback and use appreciation and recognition in their day-to-day activities, such as hosting meetings and working alongside the team.

Hosting your first departmental or organizational peopling meeting will also be met with many questions and uncertainty around the expectations and purpose of this meeting from your leaders. I am not always a fan of pre-meetings, but this is one example where a pre-meeting could be beneficial. Bringing all the attendees together several weeks before the peopling meeting and reviewing the agenda in detail is an important step. Be sure to review what prework they must have completed and what they may need to consider for the discussions in advance of the meeting; again, it is a valuable use of time and will help ensure your first peopling meeting gets off to a great start. Your people are the most valuable part of the organization, so ensuring everyone is clear about the expectations, anticipated outcomes, and ground rules will serve you well.

Finally, when it comes to changing or introducing formalized awards and recognition programs, it's an excellent idea to find ways to involve the entire organization in planning which award categories fit your company best. It sounds like an extra step that will take more time out of already jam-packed days, but the more you involve your team in important culture-building activities such as this one, the more connected to the vision they will be. You could use two tactics to gather their feedback and opinions, neither of which are overly time-consuming. The first would be to host one or two focus groups, depending on the size of your organization, with the middle leaders. Compile their ideas with the ideas of the senior leadership team and then build an all-team-member survey asking them to rank or vote for their favorites. It's always a good idea to ask open-ended questions about any ideas they might have that were not a part of the survey. You'll be surprised by the creativity that can come from your frontline team members if you simply take the time to engage with them on how they want to be recognized; it is well worth the effort.

Changing your organization's culture will be difficult, no matter how you try to spin it, but you can do things to make it easier for the organization and its people. Remember, many of your team will welcome all the ways you are trying to change. People want to be appreciated, recognized, and developed, and they want to know there are opportunities to grow their skills and careers in your organization. The most significant change required in this culture shift will be a change in your leadership teams, specifically, how they think and behave. So remember to create as many opportunities as possible for them to experience the new ways of being in advance of your change date and celebrate their wins early and often. Once the change is in motion, it will help ensure a positive experience that will last into the future. Engaging the organization's leaders is crucial. Without their support and role modeling, it will be next to impossible to rally the rest of the troops, so engage them early in the change planning process and communicate, communicate, communicate. And when you think you've communicated enough, repeat the message ten more times. It's incredible how often you need to relay important change messages before they become part of your everyday working culture.

Choosing to lead people is one of the most significant career choices you'll make. It's an important job that comes with tremendous responsibility, and to really do it justice, you must understand that you hold people's livelihoods and career potential in your hands, not to mention the power you have to create either a positive and happy workplace for your team or one that is toxic and sends people home feeling anxious, frustrated, or depressed.

So, in closing, I wish you all the very best on this tremendously important leadership journey you're about to set out on. Your leadership is absolutely vital to creating the kind of culture that people want to come to work in every day. Be courageous and make the type of bold changes required to protect and nurture the well-being of your team. In doing so, you'll be rewarded with their support, hard work, and, of course, loyalty.

ACKNOWLEDGMENTS

I would not have been able to write this book without the love and unwavering support I have received from my family and friends:

Jimmy, I couldn't have done this without your support and encouragement. Not just with this book but in so many aspects of our journey together. Here's to our next chapter.

Mum, Dad, Mitch & Tammi, Chris & Connor, you've always been in my corner. Because of you, I have the values and principles I do, and because of your love and support, I can live them out every day.

Allison, Brita, Erin, Kristen, Kristy, Sandra, and Tracy, you ladies are the best friends a girl could ever ask for. Thank you for cheering me on, picking me up, and loving and supporting me every step of the way.

Mom, Ken & Jarka, you love me like I am your own daughter. Your continuous support and encouragement mean the world to me.

I'm incredibly grateful to all the leaders I've had in my career that took the time to teach me through their example:

Joanne Forrester, you come first for obvious reasons. I learned more from you and your example in the four years we worked together than any other leader I had. You pushed me to be the very best leader I could be. #ladygrit

Jordan Holm, you taught me about balancing the need for action with the need for empathy. Your calm, steady, and caring leadership during COVID-19 and its impact on our industry is engrained in me forever. Not to mention your impressive grittiness!!!

Cheryl & Jim Treliving, you are examples of leaders who put people first. You always took the time to check in with me, especially during some difficult times for my family, and you continually showed me how much you appreciated me and the work I was doing. You always made me feel connected to and inspired by the Boston Pizza brand.

Caroline Ternes, you embody all that Starbucks is, and working for you marked the best example of coaching and appreciative leadership I've experienced. You cared enough to give me the honest feedback that helped shape me into the leader I am today.

Connie Officer, my first mentor, I always admired your strength and dedication to operational excellence; you showed me that hard work and attention to detail always pays off. I am so thankful for the interest you took in my development at such an impressionable time in my career.

Gina Buchanan, you were my first and favorite leadership instructor at BCIT. You sparked in me a lifelong journey toward leadership development. You inspired me to follow in your footsteps and complete my Master's Degree in Leadership at Royal Roads; you had such a tremendous impact on me and my leadership approach.

Kristy Richards, Mark Barkey, Mark Cowl, Jon Chiu & Cory Goddard, and the entire Operations Team at Boston Pizza International, you were the best and brightest team I ever had the privilege to lead. You taught me so much about myself as a leader and what we can accomplish together when we focus on each other's needs above our own. I'm also so very thankful for your patience with all my "social experiments!"

Cara Piggot, I don't know of many senior leaders that would embark on a six-month transition of the BP dream team with me as you did. You're a colleague that became a mentor and a friend. Thank you from the bottom of my heart.

The Starbucks Original 8 + Sherwin—Wilson, Jones, Helen, Isao, Cheryl, Jason, Amanda & Mark, I'll never forget my time in our original district. You taught me so much about leadership and the incredible Starbucks experience. NOLA!!!

APPENDICES

Download these complimentary resources and more at www.thegreatresignationtoolkit.com.

Appendix A—Sample New Team Member Training Checklist

Training Checklist	Trainer	Completed	Notes
Role Specific Tools			
SKYPE for Business			
Company Intranet			
One Note			
Daily Management Tasks			
Setting Up an Office Day			
Time Management			
Administration Activities			
Review our Organizational Chart			
Submitting Vacation Requests			
Office Tour			
Set Up Laptop & Phone			
Intranet Tour			
Crisis Communication Plan			
Health and Safety			
Standard Operating Procedures			

NOTES:

Team Member Sign-Off   Manager Sign Off

Name: Name:

Appendix B—Sample 360 Performance Review Stakeholder Feedback Form

360 Performance Review Stakeholder Feedback

Stakeholder Name & Department:

Team Member Name:

Department & Position:

Date:

STEP	STAKEHOLDER FEEDBACK
CONTINUE	Summary of areas they excel in that they should 'continue' doing in their role and perhaps could be shared with others in the same position. *List as many as are mentioned.*
	1. 2. 3.
START	Summary of actions they could 'start' doing in their role that would greatly benefit the organization and/or their relationships. *List as many as are mentioned.*
	1. 2. 3.
STOP	Summary of actions or behaviors they could 'stop' doing in their role that do not add any value to the organization or their relationships. List as many as are mentioned.
	1. 2. 3.

Appendix C—Sample Self-Performance Review Form

Self-Performance Review

Name & Position:

Department:

Date:

	SELF-PERFORMANCE REVIEW FEEDBACK
CONTINUE	List actions and behaviors that you excel at in your position.
	1. 2.
START	List actions and behaviors that you could incorporate into your position to enhance your overall performance, effectiveness, or relationships.
	1. 2.
STOP	List any limiting actions or behaviors detracting from your overall performance or effectiveness in the role.
	1. 2.

INDIVIDUALS COMMENTS & KEY SUCCESSES:

Appendix D—Sample 360 Performance Review: Final Assessment

360 Performance Review

Name & Position:

Department & Leader:

Date:

	SUMMARY OF 360 PERFORMANCE REVIEW FEEDBACK
CONTINUE	Summary of the 'CONTINUE' themes in team members' feedback – *not limited to three*
	1. 2. 3.
START	Summary of the 'START' themes in the team members' feedback - *not limited to three*
	1. 2. 3.
STOP	Summary of the 'STOP' themes in the team members' feedback - *not limited to three*
	1. 2. 3.

LEADERS COMMENTS:

Appendix E—Sample
Supplementary Training Plan

Supplemental Training Plan

Name:

Department:

Date & Duration of Plan:

Proposed Training	Business Need to be Solved	Resources and Support Required	Timeline

Appendix F—Sample Performance Improvement Plan

Performance Improvement Plan (PIP) Confidential

Name & Position:

Leader & Department:

Date:

This Performance Improvement Plan (PIP) aims to define areas of concern and gaps in your work performance, reiterate the expectations of xxx, and allow you the opportunity to demonstrate improvement and commitment.

Areas of Concern:

1.
2.
3.

Observations, Previous Discussions, or Counseling:

While previous informal discussions have taken place, this will serve as our first official document of your performance and the need for immediate and sustained improvement.

Improvement Goals:

These are the goals related to areas of concern to be improved and addressed:

1.	
2.	
3.	

Follow-Up Updates: You will receive feedback on your progress according to the following schedule:

Date Scheduled	Activity	Conducted By	Completion Date

Timeline for Improvement, Consequences & Expectations:

Signatures:

Employee Signature:

Date:

Supervisor/Manager Signature:

Date:

Appendix G—Sample Team Member Development Plan

Professional Development Plan

Name & Position:
Leader & Department:
Duration of Development Plan:

Knowledge, skills, and abilities to be developed: **(Suggest a maximum of three goals here.)**

1.
2.

Developmental Goal #1: summary of knowledge, skill, or ability to be developed here. *Suggest no more than three activities for each developmental goal.*
- **Developmental Activity—**
- **Application in Role Activity—**

Developmental Goal #2: summary of knowledge, skill, or ability to be developed here. *Suggest no more than three activities for each developmental goal.*
- ***Developmental Activity—***
- **Application in Role Activity—**

Appendix H—Sample Culture Survey Questions

Culture Survey: All Team Members

1. Our company culture values integrity, teamwork, and collaboration. Do you think these words accurately describe your experience working as part of this team?

2. I can fulfill all my duties and maintain a healthy work-life balance—*rank from never to always.*

3. I feel the organization listens to me and my ideas are usually at least considered—*rank from never to always.*

4. The organization has provided me with learning and development opportunities that have helped me advance my career and gain new skills—*rank from never to always.*

5. What kind of learning and development opportunities would you like to see in the future?

6. I can see myself working as a part of this organization for the long term—*rank from very likely to unlikely.*

7. The organization is true to its values; everyone is treated with respect and dignity—*rank from strongly disagree to agree strongly.*

8. My leaders provide me with constructive feedback that helps me learn and grow—*rank from strongly disagree to agree strongly.*

9. I feel my accomplishments are regularly recognized by my peers and leaders—rank from strongly disagree to agree strongly.

10. I look forward to coming to work every day—*rank from strongly disagree to agree strongly.*

Appendix I—Sample Skip Level Questions

Skip Level Questions

Skip-level meetings allow senior leaders to understand their organization at a deeper level. It's a chance for them to spend time with team members in the organization they wouldn't usually work closely with. Hearing what's going well and what needs work from the "ground up" can help senior leaders prioritize problems and celebrate successes.

- What projects at work have you most enjoyed working on?
- What is some good news you'd like to share?
- What is the biggest issue facing your role in the organization?
- If there was one thing you could "fix" in the company, what would it be?
- How would you change things if you were in my shoes?
- Would you recommend working here to your friends? Why or why not?
- What is keeping you from being more successful than you already are?
- How can we help you achieve those goals?
- What would you do differently if you were the manager of your team?
- Do you know the company's goals?
- What can we do to make you happy with your role?
- What do you need from the leadership team?

- Do you know how your team's goals support the company?
- Is there anything else we should have discussed?
- Is there anything else I can do to help you and your team?
- How can we help you work with your manager?
- What is your favorite/least favorite part of the company?
- When have you felt most proud of being part of this organization?

Appendix J—Sample Stay Interview Questions

Stay Interview Questions

Ensuring your team members are happy and satisfied with their working environment is an essential part of your retention strategy. These questions can help to provide insight into your team members' experience on your team and what you, as their leader, can do to help them feel valued while supporting their ongoing development.

1. What about your job excites you most to come to work each day?
2. What makes you want to stay home?
3. What aspects of your job do you like the most and the least?
4. What would make you leave (our company) for another job?
5. Do you feel appreciated and recognized by your leader and your team?
6. What kind of recognition do you find most meaningful?

ABOUT THE AUTHOR

Laura Darrell is a former leadership executive with over twenty-five years of senior leadership experience at some of the world's most esteemed brands, including Starbucks and Apple. She regularly contributes to the *Franchise Wire* and Franchising. com, where she writes about the collaborative leadership skills required to lead a franchised organization. Laura holds a Master's Degree in Organizational Leadership from Royal Roads University in British Columbia, Canada. There, she conducted her thesis research on multi-disciplinary collaborative leadership practices that enhance business results for all key stakeholders. She is the author of two other books: *The Promotability Gap* and *The Principles of Franchisee Success*. Laura currently resides in Mexico City.

ENDNOTES

PART ONE: WHY THEY LEAVE

1   Vesoulis, Abby. "Why Literally Millions of Americans Are Quitting Their Jobs." *Time*, 13 Oct. 2021, https://time.com/6106322/the-great-resignation-jobs/.

2   Cass, Oren. "The Labour Shortage Myth." *The Atlantic*, 2 Jun. 2023, https://www.theatlantic.com/ideas/archive/2023/06/labor-shortage-low-unemployment.

3   Asheesh, Moosapeta. "Low Unemployment & High Participation Rate Indicate Tight Labour Market." *CICNews*, 23 Oct. 2023, https://www.cicnews.com/2023/10/low-unemployment-and-high-participation-rate.

4   Schwartz, Emma. "The Global Healthcare Worker Shortage: 10 Numbers to Note." *Project Hope*, 6 Apr. 2022, https://www.projecthope.org/the-global-health-worker-shortage-10-numbers-to-note/04/2022/.

5   Lewis, Nicole. "IT Workers Will be Hard to Find and Keep in 2022." *SHRM*, 13 Dec. 2021, https://www.shrm.org/

resourcesandtools/hr-topics/technology/pages/it-workers-will-be-hard-find-keep-2022.aspx.

6 Flynn, Jack. "23 Recruitment Statistics." *Zippiacareerexpert.com,* 23 Feb. 2023, https://www.zippia.com/advice/recruitment-statistics/.

7 Writes, Aurora. "These are the Companies with the Lowest Turnover." 11 Jul. 2022, https://smithindex.wilsonema.com/these-are-the-companies-with-the-lowest-employee-turnover/.

8 Taylor, Bill. "How One Fastfood Chain Keeps its Turnover Absurdly Low." *Harvard Business Review,* 26 Jan. 2016, https://hbr.org/2016/01/how-one-fast-food-chain-keeps-its-turnover-rates-absurdly-low.

9 Lee, Charles. "Four Communications Solutions for Restaurant Turnover." *Modern Restaurant Manager*, 21 Nov. 2021, https://modernrestaurantmanagement.com/four-communications-solutions-to-fast-food-turnover/.

10 Deloitte. "The Deloitte Global 2022 Millennial & Gen Z Survey." *Deloitte Global*, 18 May 2022, https://www2.deloitte.com/content/dam/Deloitte/global/Documents/deloitte-2022-genz-millennial-survey.pdf.

CHAPTER 1: A LACK OF CAREER OPPORTUNITIES

11 Hamilton, Kelly, Sandhu Reetu, M.S, & Ph.D., Hamill, Laura, Ph.D. "The Science of Care." Limeade Institute, Sept. 2019, https://www.limeade.com/wpcontent/uploads/2019/09/LimeadeInstitute_TheScienceOfCare_Whitepaper_Web.pdf.

12 Adkins, Amy, Rigoni, Brandon. "Millennials Want Jobs to be Development Opportunities." Gallup. 30 Jun. 2016, https://www.gallup.com/workplace/236438/millennials-jobs-development-opportunities.aspx.

13 Jenkins, Ryan. "Gen Z Wants This More Than Flexibility at Work." LinkedIn, 12 Apr. 2022, https://www.linkedin.com/pulse/gen-z-wants-more-than-flexibility-work-ryan-jenkins-csp/.

14 ADP Blog. "Internal vs. External Hires: Pros, Cons and Considerations." ADP HR Blog, 3 Jul. 2017, https://sbshrs.adpinfo.com/blog/internal-vs-external-hires-pros-cons-considerations.

15 David, Tallulah. "29 Surprising Stats on Employer Branding". Career Arc, 13 Nov. 2017, https://www.careerarc.com/blog/employer-branding-study-infographic.

CHAPTER 2: NO INVESTMENT IN EMPLOYEE DEVELOPMENT

16 M. Maria. "28 Interesting Employee Training Statistics." Leftronic, 4 Dec. 2020, https://leftronic.com/blog/employee-training-statistics/.

17 O'Donnell, Rita. "Managers say they lack training, 44% feel overwhelmed at work." *HRDive*, 3 Apr. 2018, https://www.hrdive.com/news/managers-say-they-lack-training-and-44-feel-overwhelmed-at-work/520396/.

18 Gifford, Thomas. "People Leave because of Poor Leadership." Leadership First, 27 Dec. 2021, https://www.leadershipfirst.net/post/people-leave-because-of-poor-leadership.

19 Ryba, Kristin. "What is Employee Engagement? What, Why, and How to Improve It." *Quantum Workplace*, 21, Mar. 2021, https://www.quantumworkplace.com/future-of-work/what-is-employee-engagement.

20 Townsend, Cat. "Why Consistency is the Key to Business Success." *The Good Alliance*, Dec. 2019, https://thegoodalliance.org/articles/consistency-key-to-business-success/.

21 Gutierrez, Karla. "Mind-blowing Statistics Prove the Value of Employee Training." *Shift eLearning*, https://thegoodalliance.org/articles/consistency-key-to-business-success/.

22 Adkins, Amy, Rigoni, Brandon. "Millennials Want Jobs to be Development Opportunities." Gallup. 30 Jun. 2016, https://www.gallup.com/workplace/236438/millennials-jobs-development-opportunities.aspx.

23 Janzer, Cinnamon. "The Gen Z Workforce: Who They Are, and What They Want." Workest (zenefits.com), 20 May 2021, https://www.zenefits.com/workest/the-gen-z-workforce-who-they-are-and-what-they-want.

24 Admin. "The True Cost of Not Providing Employee Training." *Shift E-learning (shiftelearning.com),* Jun. 2021, https://www.shiftelearning.com/blog/the-true-cost-of-not-providing-employee-training.

25 Admin. "The True Cost of Not Providing Employee Training." *Shift E-learning (shiftelearning.com),* Jun. 2021, https://www.shiftelearning.com/blog/the-true-cost-of-not-providing-employee-training.

26 Admin. "The True Cost of Not Providing Employee Training." *Shift E-learning (shiftelearning.com),* Jun. 2021, https://www.

shiftelearning.com/blog/the-true-cost-of-not-providing-employee-training.

CHAPTER 3: MIDDLE MANAGERS LACK LEADERSHIP TRAINING

27   Hancock, Brian, Schaninger, Bill. "The Vanishing Middle Manager." McKinsey & Company, 5 Feb. 2021, https://www.mckinsey.com/business-functions/people-and-organizational-performance/our-insights/the-vanishing-middle-manager.

28   Hogan, Maren. "Top 5 Reasons Why People Quit Bosses, Not Their Jobs." *LinkedIn*, 11 Mar. 2015, https://www.linkedin.com/pulse/top-5-reasons-why-people-quit-bosses-jobs-maren-hogan/.

CHAPTER 4: SENIOR LEADERS ARE DISCONNECTED

29   Golis, Chris. "How to tell if you're suffering from CEO disease." *Smart Company*, 29 Nov. 2012, https://www.smartcompany.com.au/people-human-resources/professional-development/how-to-tell-if-youre-suffering-from-ceo-disease/.

30   Workday. "Businesses 'Out of Touch' With Employees Working From Home, Peakon Reveals." *PR Newswire*, 21 May 2020, https://www.prnewswire.com/news-releases/businesses-out-of-touch-with-employees-working-from-home-peakon-reveals-301063890.html.

[31] Lund, Annika. "Bad managers cause poor health." Karolinska Institute (ki.se) 2016, https://ki.se/en/research/bad-managers-cause-poor-health.

CHAPTER 5: EMPLOYEES FEEL UNDERVALUED

[32] Mann, Annamarie, Dvorak, Nate. "Employee Recognition: Low Cost, High Impact." Gallup, 28 Jun. 2016, https://news.gallup.com/businessjournal/193238/employee-recognition-low-cost-high-impact.aspx.

[33] Lipman, Victor. "66% Of Employees Would Quit If They Feel Unappreciated." *Forbes*, 15 Apr. 2017, https://www.forbes.com/sites/victorlipman/2017/04/15/66-of-employees-would-quit-if-they-feel-unappreciated/?sh=7eb14b336897.

[34] Nordstrom, Todd. "79 Percent of Employees Quit Because They're not Appreciated. Try These 4 Things Before You Say Good-Bye." Inc.com, 19 Sept. 2017. https://www.inc.com/todd-nordstrom/79-percent-of-employees-quit-because-theyre-not-ap.html.

[35] Psychology. "The Need for Recognition, Cornerstone of Self-Esteem." *Exploring Your Mind*, 18 Jan. 2016, https://exploringyourmind.com/need-recognition-cornerstone-self-esteem/.

[36] Kinne, Aaron. "Learn the Importance and What the Benefits of Employee Recognition are in 2022." *Workhuman*, 2022, https://www.workhuman.com/resources/employee-recognition/benefits-of-employee-recognition.

[37] Biro M. Meghan. "Happy Employees = Hefty Profits." Forbes, 19 Jan. 2014, https://www.forbes.com/sites/meghanbiro/2014/01/19/happy-employees-hefty-profits/?sh=56da495221a8.

38 Admin. "Generational Preferences of Employee Recognition." MTM Recognition, 16 Jan. 2020, https://mtmrecognition.com/2020/01/generational-preferences-of-employee-recognition/.

39 Glazer, Robert. "'Command and Control' Leadership Is Dead. Here's What's Taking Its Place." Inc.com, 12 Aug. 2019, https://www.inc.com/robert-glazer/command-control-leadership-is-dead-heres-whats-taking-its-place.html.

40 Miller, Stephen. "Generation Z and Millennials Seek Recognition at Work." SHMR.org, 12 Sept. 2019, https://www.shrm.org/resourcesandtools/hr-topics/benefits/pages/generation-z-and-millennials-seek-recognition-at-work.aspx.

41 Forleo, Marie. "Why You Need Clarity to Achieve Your Goals." SUCCESS, 9 Jan. 2020, https://www.success.com/why-you-need-clarity-to-achieve-your-goals/.

CHAPTER 6: A TOXIC WORKING CULTURE

42 Sull, David, Sull, Charles, Zweig, Ben. "Toxic Culture Is Driving the Great Resignation." *MIT Sloan*, 11 Jan. 2022, https://sloanreview.mit.edu/article/toxic-culture-is-driving-the-great-resignation/.

43 Dujay, Jon. "Toxic culture top reason for turnover, according to research." *HRD New Zealand*, 1 Feb. 2022, https://www.hcamag.com/nz/specialisation/mental-health/toxic-culture-top-reason-for-turnover-according-to-research/323665.

44 Zak, J. Paul. "The Neuroscience of Trust." *Harvard Business Review*, Jan-Feb. 2017, https://hbr.org/2017/01/the-neuroscience-of-trust.

PART TWO: CLOSING THE CULTURE GAP

45   Stahl, Ashley. "The Compensation Package Gen-Z And Millennials Want." Forbes, 15 Sept. 2020, https://www.forbes.com/sites/ashleystahl/2020/09/15/the-compensation-package-gen-z-and-millennials-want/?sh=528da51e1753.

CHAPTER 7: A STRONG START

46   Taylor, Tess. "Why do 28% of employees quit in their first 90 days? Poor onboarding practices." HR Dive, 25 Apr. 2017, https://www.hrdive.com/news/why-do-28-of-employees-quit-in-their-first-90-days-poor-onboarding-practi/441139/.

47   Marone, Mark. "Why Purpose-Driven Organizations Matter." *Dale Carnegie*, 31 Jul. 2020, https://www.dalecarnegie.com/blog/does-having-an-organizational-purpose-really-matter/.

48   Haessler, Arlene. "Tell, Show, Do and Review. A Useful Tool for Trainers and Instructors." *Arlene Haessler Information Science Graduate Student*, Feb. 2016, https://ahaessler.wixsite.com/online-resume-cv/single-post/2016/02/21/tell-show-do-review-a-useful-tool-for-trainers-and-instructors.

CHAPTER 8: MANAGING PERFORMANCE AND DEVELOPING TALENT

49   HR Base Camp. "One-on-One Meetings Are a Manager's Most Powerful Engagement Tool." CEDR HR Solutions, 23 Feb. 2022, https://www.cedrsolutions.com/manager-one-on-one-meetings-with-employees/.

50   Kearney, Audrey, Hamel, Liz, Brodie, Mollyann. "Mental Health Impact of the COVID-19 Pandemic: An Update." Kaiser Family Foundation, 14 Apr. 2021, https://www.kff.org/coronavirus-covid-19/poll-finding/mental-health-impact-of-the-covid-19-pandemic/.

51   Schleckser, Jim. "How Many Direct Reports Should You Have?" *Inc.com*, 5 Mar. 2019, https://www.inc.com/jim-schleckser/how-many-direct-reports-should-you-have.html.

CHAPTER 9: COACHING LEADERSHIP

52   Briggs, Teresa, Michelle, Kerrick, Trenaglio, Tamika. "Publication: Elevating Future Leaders." Deloitte US, ND, https://www2.deloitte.com/us/en/pages/about-deloitte/articles/elevating-future-leaders.html.

CHAPTER 10: APPRECIATIVE LEADERSHIP

53   Coker, Diana. "Employee recognition drives retention and productivity." HR Digest, 17 Jul. 2021, https://www.thehrdigest.com/employee-recognition-drives-retention-and-productivity/.

54   Nink, Marco, Robinson, Jennifer. "Add Team Praise to Your Employee Recognition Toolkit." Gallup, 9 Feb. 2021, https://www.gallup.com/workplace/329351/add-team-praise-employee-recognition-toolkit.aspx.

55   MHA. "Mental Health and COVID-19: Two Years After the Pandemic, Mental Health Concerns Continue to Increase." *Mental Health America*, Apr. 2022, https://mhanational.org/mental-health-and-covid-19-two-years-after-pandemic.

CHAPTER 11: LEADERSHIP ACCOUNTABILITY

[56] Grensing-Pophal, Lin. "Stay vs. Exit Interviews and Why Each Is Important." HR Daily Advisor, 20 Feb. 2020, https://hrdailyadvisor.blr.com/2020/02/20/stay-vs-exit-interviews-and-why-each-is-important/.

CHAPTER 12: CHANGE LEADERSHIP

[57] Antliff, Sara. "What causes change fatigue and how to overcome it." Atlassian, 28 Jun. 2021, https://www.atlassian.com/blog/leadership/change-fatigue.

[58] Poleo, Dr. Geri. "The No Man's Land of Change: The Paradox of Change and Stability." Change Management Solutions, ND, https://changewithoutburnout.com/2018/07/17/the-no-mans-land-of-change-the-paradox-of-change-and-stability/.